A Life Coach's Journey Through Darkness to Light

There are no right or wrongs in life as long as you learn

by

Kelly Keith certified and licensed
Spiritual Happiness life coach

DORRANCE
PUBLISHING CO
EST. 1920
PITTSBURGH, PENNSYLVANIA 15238

Dorrance Publishing Co
585 Alpha Drive
Pittsburgh, PA 15238
Visit our website at www.dorrancebookstore.com

ISBN: 979-8-8868-3058-3
eISBN: 979-8-8868-3922-7

TABLE OF CONTENTS

IN THE BEGINNING
EARLY YEARS

I was born 1980 in Montclair California. I was raised in Upland, California. At the age of two I was run over by a car and died and was revived at the scene. Only the first set of tires went over me. My uncle Tim had rescued me from the other set of tires going over me. So, my start here on earth wasn't a perfect one, but I did get a settlement from that case at the age of two—$10,000 put into a bank account. I couldn't touch the money 'til I was eighteen years old, but I knew the value of money at a very young age.

Probably at five years old I knew I had a lot of money. My whole family made it very clear and made me aware of my financial value in their eyes. So, I guess that was the universe's way of letting me know I will never be without money whether I work hard for it or not because of good deeds from past lives, I obviously in this lifetime karmically will never go without. That is what I discovered just recently from a past life regression.

My parents got divorced when I was ten years old. My mom moved me and my brothers to Gresham, Oregon when I was twelve. By the time I was fourteen years old, I was too cool for school. My freshman year I hardly went to school. I had to work extra night classes to graduate because I really didn't care about school. It couldn't hold my attention My first job was McDonald's at the age of sixteen. I graduated in 1998 in Eugene, Oregon. My story was like the normal kid from the past up until that point. You know, like I had to take a bus to a train then an hour on the train in the rain in the snow to get to school. I'm cracking up right now it's true, though. That's why I didn't always get there. Me and my brother Brian, my older brother, would ditch school. I was the middle child of three.

I had two biological brothers, the younger was Jonathan. We were all three years apart. I was the only girl. Let me go back a few years when I was in elementary school. I loved school back then. I loved being on stage I even did choir till my senior year in high school. I never wanted to miss a day of school in elementary school. I always wanted to get the award for never missing a day of school. One reason was because I could get on the stage. I liked being the center of attention when I was young. I sold candy bars in elementary school and every year I would win the biggest prize for selling the most candy bars four years in a row or fundraising packages every year for a good four-year streak. Every year I would win the biggest prize. Well, one year a boy got upset because of me winning. It was my last year trying real hard in third grade, eight years old, and the prize was a black-and-white TV/radio AM/FM. A little boy pushed me down after school one day in front of the school. I hit my head on my Rainbow Brite lunchbox; they were plastic back then.

I woke up in the nurses office. My mom was really upset. I was told the little boy was jealous. Moving on a couple years, I was put in beauty pageants. I became Miss American Starlet and won queen of San Bernadino County twice at age ten and eleven years old. Two years in a row I won Miss American Starlet. I also went to the national pageant both years in Palm Springs. The first year I won top 10 out of 100 girls, the second year, I did not win anything at the nationals. My winning streak had ended. That was the year of the divorce. I actually cried that year for the first time after not winning because I knew the stress and the money that was put into the pageant affected me on a big level. I didn't ever understand why the girls would cry when they didn't win because I had never experienced it but that year I did. My mom would tell me (well, a lotta money gets put into the whole experience) she said so the girls feel the disappointment when they don't win, but you were never not one to feel that because I had never lost yet. I didn't understand the first year, but I did that year; and I didn't want to compete ever again after that. With anything in my life, competition was out of the question.

Also, out of my personality. I no longer wanted to compete or to be better than anybody else. Little did I know at that time, my life was about to take a turn. Don't get me wrong, I don't regret anything in my life, but I am glad that now I am aware of this with an extensive amount of self-discovery, research, a past life regression, and years of making bad choices. Then I was able to see how my inner child was limiting me because of that experience way back then and I discovered my purpose. So now I'm gonna take you on a journey from the dark side of my life that followed.

I started smoking cigarettes at twelve years old trying to impress a girlfriend that I had just met from my new school in seventh grade in Gresham, Oregon. In 1992 you could smoke in the malls. We went to the mall together and I pretended like I had always smoked just to fit in with her and I smoked like I was a pro. It looked like I had been doing it for years even though it was my first cigarette. I did not cough at all. I went on a journey after that experimenting with drugs. I feel because I was open to the cigarettes, I was open to trying weed after as well and acid tabs only 4X I (fried) as it was called and drinking hard liquor on weekends at my older boyfriend's house. I feel me not wanting to compete in anything or be challenged in any way was the gateway to my choices of friends and choices of the drug exploration.

I'm most certain from my perception if I would've continued with competing and selling things and fundraising I would've done cheerleading maybe continued with the pageants I wouldn't have gone down the road that I did to get to where I am right now. I know everything happens for a reason. I'm finding out everything is kind of a domino effect. I'm gonna say this a couple times throughout the book—you can take a slow boat to China or you can take the jet. Free will says you get to choose, but the ultimate outcome, I'm finding out, will be the same either way you can just get to your ultimate happiness faster or you can take a more challenging way with more obstacles, more people, places, and things to experience through this matrix.

The contracts that we signed and agreed to before we came was with the inner knowing and awareness that we were going to enjoy the journey with all the ups and downs and cause and affect positive or negative experiences but ultimately the outcome will be the same. Fast forward back to high school leaving my middle school exploration.

So, my junior year I had gotten a job at McDonald's. Sixteen years old. My brother was a manager. I went to school from eight in the morning 'til eight at night, then I would go to work until midnight and then do it all again, Monday through Friday just to graduate my senior year. I met a man when I was seventeen—my first husband. I was head over heels for him. Every girl wanted to be with him. Every guy wanted to be him. Our relationship was really public in that small town Eugene, Oregon. I had a lot of responsibilities for a seventeen-year-old. My car insurance, my personal phone line in my room. I had a bank account. We had pagers back then, and I also paid for my own gas for my 77 Datsun pickup truck, which my brother later flipped. He fell asleep while driving, and then we just shared his Toyota Tercel.

I'd like to say that my first husband was a love story, but I ran away from home on a Halloween night in my costume because my mom was going to ground me for staying out too late. I was dating a twenty-six-year-old who became my first husband when I was seventeen and about to be a senior in high school. My mom thought he was twenty-one. I didn't think the twenty-six-year-old was going to wait for me to be ungrounded. (I'm saying twenty-six-year-old instead of his name but you know who you are.) So I decided not to go home. My mom kept all my clothes until my senior year. I didn't even have underwear because it was Halloween night when I decided to run away. I had to wear his clothes to school 'til he sold a watch and got me some clothes. I was a year from turning eighteen, which was only for one year and then my mom gave them back.

I graduated high school barely—straight Ds. I worked hard for those Ds. Fast forward thirty days before we married at my age of nineteen. He made a decision when we were broken up one weekend to get drunk and him and a friend stole a Rolex from a college party he went to. They got caught. He was court ordered to turn himself in and do thirteen months in prison. we got married before he went to turn himself in. I'm gonna spare you the drama before he went in, we had lived together for two years at that time of our relationship. I waited for him for a thirteen-month prison term. At the beginning of the thirteen months, I had an ex come back to me, my first love, who told me about getting an annulment.

Also, I had just found out that morning at work at Bon Marche, which is just a different name for a Macy's, a girl confessed to me that they did have sex the last time we were broken up, which I felt that was unforgivable at the time. I felt tricked into marriage before he went to turn himself in. I told him if I had known he had sexual relations with her, I wouldn't have wanted to marry him. So my ex was explaining to me what an annulment was. I didn't even know what that was up until that point. My first love that night got stabbed because that was the thing that he liked to do when he got drunk—getting into fights Whether that be at a party or at a bar. Well, this time my ex (first love) he refused to go to the hospital, so I got convinced by his brother to go over that night and talk him into going to the hospital. Instead, I went over there and doctored him up and then smoked weed because he still refused to go and we had sex. This was at the beginning of my husband's prison term. I was vulnerable; no excuse. I did sleep with him, but then I realized I wanted to wait for my husband, that my ex was a cheater and I couldn't forgive at that time so that's what I did. I stopped talking to my ex and waited faithfully the rest of the thirteen months with the intent at the time to deny, deny, deny if I ever was asked or if it was ever discovered somehow, because I was already a great pathological liar anyway.

I had to lie. My mom was very strict. I was taught to lie because she was so strict. If I wanted any freedom in my life, which I desired and still do today very strongly, and the same goes for any other young adult that had strict parents. Don't let people fool you. My ex almost had me convinced to get an annulment. I'm thankful for the way it all turned out today. I was working four jobs—one was McDonald's, housekeeping for the Merry Maids, I had my own housekeeping clients on the side, also babysitting for my older stepsister. Then my Ford Explorer exploded on me. While he was in jail, I came up with an idea—because I lost all those jobs because my car broke down—to be a stripper. I had a girlfriend that helped support my confidence to do that I found a strip club forty-five minutes out of town, which ended up being too far for me.

And then I came up with the idea to work at

a strip club nearby my house off of Highway 99 it was called the (Bush Company) back then. The first day I made $300 in four hours that was more than I made at McDonald's with two weeks of my pay. I was hooked. I got sucked into fast cash so quickly and now my dark-side story really is beginning.

Let me add in here real quick; you know that saying "you can't turn a hoe into a housewife"? Well, at this point, I was a housewife before I was a hoe and later I discovered it's the same the other way around as well (you can't turn a housewife into a hoe) either. THIS IS so funny. So, it's 1999. I'm nineteen years old now. I was drinking tequila straight out of the bottle and chasing it with lemon juice, visiting my husband every Sunday no matter what. Every weekend for thirteen months it was a three-hour drive and I'd lie to his face about what I was doing for work. Every weekend. I saw him more than my brother saw his long-distance girl-friend that only lived two hours away from us. I was dedicated and feeling very guilty. I never thought that I would ever become a stripper. My morals and values didn't match up, but my body did, my looks did. It wasn't until my ex during one of our breakups before he went to prison had sex with a stripper that I had become interested in that life because he was a twenty-seven-year-old man that had never stepped foot into a strip club.

All of a sudden, we break up and he was having sex with a stripper, which really piqued my interest! I wanted to know what it was that got him to do such a thing also at the same time I wanted to be like those girls too and learn how to bring it home to him so he didn't go into the strip clubs anymore without me anyway. So that's where my interest grew and I always said at that point that if I ever got to the point where I was desperate enough and needed income, if I still had it in my looks and my body and had the confidence, then I would do it. Continuing from earlier with what I was saying, I went from the relationship with my mom being strict to being with a controlling Indian man, so I wasn't really free to be truly who I was. I think that was a reason I got with that older man because I kind of feared being truly free because of what was inside of me wanting to break free (the wild child).

I feel because I knew I was in a controlling situation but I also knew that it helped me to be a good girl, at least what I felt was good from my perception. I did want to be a good girl, but I also wanted to be bad… secretly, I guess. So, you see, I had strong values and morals and that's exactly what any girl should ask herself before doing something such as taking her clothes off for money: Do my values and morals match the action I'm about to take? Will I still be happy with myself at the end of the day. Will I be able to look myself in a mirror and still love myself? YEP! lol

So, in Chapter 2, I will be discussing further about the game, the "stripping for dollars" game. Let me continue with what happened with my first husband. He was asking me what I had learned from us breaking up. I didn't know right away. It took me six months, but I learned never to lie, to always be honest, never do anything you can't repeat, if you're doing something you can't repeat, you shouldn't be doing it. So, when I first started my journey in the adult entertainment world, I took my first hard painful lesson learned to be honest no matter what. It got me into a lot of trouble because I used it with no filter. I had such a sharp tongue I kind of used it as a weapon. I was really blunt at first. Over time I learned 90% of people can't handle the truth, so I learned to tell those people the truth sugarcoated indirectly. It took me ten years to learn how to soften my deliverance of the truth. Being so honest got me in a lot of trouble. At one point, I had somebody chasing me down on the freeway wanting to kill me because of me being overly honest, but I got away.

When I was twenty years old and first started studying astrology, I was upset because I was understanding that your life is planned out for you already. It's all mapped out; there's a blueprint in your Akashic records and I was kind of upset about that because I'm really big on free will and I didn't wanna believe that it was all mapped out for us. But now that I'm older and knowing that I know nothing has helped me mature and be able to listen better. I've studied astrology and used it in my life in many different valuable ways for twenty-two years now and I've seen how this is unfolding. Now that I've matured enough to understand it more thoroughly and seen with my experience that this matrix needs some structure for it to make sense and work out for us the way it's supposed to, I have a newfound love that I wanna share with the world.

Now, about my journey so others can see for themselves that there are contracts we had before we came into these human experiences and the contracts need to be respected and understood. The world needs to wake up and understand that we're born here in this matrix with amnesia, an amnesia we agreed to, because the energy in the world at the time—where the planets were aligned—wasn't a world where people could understand being born with the knowledge of all our past lives and our spirit God source energy that we came from, and could understand having a built-in GPS system in the human bodies to help us feel our way through life. If it feels good, do more of that; if it feels bad, do less of that. Pretty simple. Today a lot more children are being born—you can look it up—that are remembering past lives because the energy has changed and it's time to wake up.

The planets have shifted. The energy is on our side. It's time to wake up to the matrix we live in, the one we chose to come and be part of, not to be miserable and struggle, but to have fun with the godlike power we have inside of us, and to enjoy our wonderful GPS system and higher self and guides that help cheer us on and guide us on our personal journey, or soul team in the unseen world. It's all real. It's time to wake up to that understanding of self-discovery and our mission is to have fun and create our own reality, find our soul tribes here on earth in the physical reality that we live in to help us on our adventures and to love to learn and learn to love!

KELLY KEITH

Who am I? Kelly Jean Keith. This is my story from darkness into light, and what that means and how I chose to become a spiritual happiness life coach and how all my life experiences added to me becoming my true self of who I've become now through all my learning lessons, all the different roads, people, places, and things that I feel you will really enjoy. I would like, while you read this book, for you to keep in your mind what you've experienced, what your heart wants and needs from you and try to understand that everything in your life happens for a reason. Try to relate and get to know me and what a spiritual happiness life coach is and if maybe you are one too? Or maybe would like to be coached by me and my team.

These are questions that you should ask yourself. Would you like to work with me to find who you are and how to be happy no matter what happens in your life? Or maybe you're experiencing stagnation in your life. If you need help moving forward from feeling lost in this world that we all agreed to come and experience, it is my mission and goal in writing this book to hopefully inspire others by you relating to my experiences, my struggles, and my challenges. That you get to know who I am and from my education and knowledge and experiences that I can help give you a jumpstart in the right direction or some movement from where you are now because of my growth, the good bad and ugly from my perception of my life. I want to be an example that you can do this as well. I'm hoping my energy and effort will inspire you to want to be better and to better accomplish your dreams or maybe learn what your comfort zone is and how you can push yourself to get outside of your comfort zone.

I can help you be more clear in your direction, finding your purpose and how to receive clarity every single day. I can use different skills that I have learned from divination tools and by my psychic abilities to help you find how to proceed by reading how I guided myself on my path. Or you contacting me by email or my website or social media. My soul consciousness is fully awakened and I'm getting to use what I learned to help others with my discoveries of self. My message in some of these chapters is going to show you there's no dark place that you cannot climb out of when you've hit bottom. There's only one way to go and that is up. We live in a new energy called Aquarian time—the new world, as we call it, the new earth that we are living.

KELLY KEITH

The collective needs to find joy because the energy that we live in now should only be about truth in love. You should look around you and only see truth and love and only be doing things that you enjoy in your life and becoming a better human Aquarian energy that is influencing us represents evolution, bettering ourselves, growth, expansion, and learning to serve others. This is the new world energy. We all need to find the light, your positive side because we are all light beings, gods and goddesses. We all have it in us. The light and the dark sides (our shadow self, Carol Jung psychiatrist from the 1900s) tells us of our architypes, and personality characteristics—the female energy and the masculine energy, the positive and the negative.

We are the creators of our own destiny. Nobody else is responsible for what you see going on in your world. It's all you, the master of your creation. If you don't like what you see, then change it. That is my message in this book. You can create whatever you want. The sky is the limit. Stop giving your personal power away to others by blaming others and making them responsible for you. Where you're at today is all you. Also, this is Kelly's Goddess Path because it truly is me chasing my own inner light, positive side through the darkness of my choices that I have achieved and got to learn from so far. I send my love and light. I hope this finds you and awakens your mind to new possibilities. There are no rights or wrongs in life. That was a message at the beginning of time that was hidden from humans because of the justice system.

There are no rights or wrongs in life because we all have different perceptions. My perception and your perception are not the same, so what I feel is wrong in my mind and your mind it would not be wrong or vice versa. The only thing that matters is if you learn from what you feel was wrong. If you learned from it, then it was never wrong to begin with. It's like a snake eating its own tail; you have to become aware of what you're doing and fix it, but if you do not experience things in full awareness, you will never be able to see the things that you are repeating in your life. The one thing we should never do is judge ourselves or others because there is no real right way to get to where you're supposed to go.

It's all about momentum. Do you wanna go faster? Do you wanna go slower to your ultimate happiness and satisfaction? Once you get tuned in, tapped in, turned on, and plugged in to your higher intelligence, the game just begins. You become the master creator of your reality and whether you feel your mistakes were good or bad, positive or negative in your life you will enjoy all the contrast that life experiences hand you.

ADULT ENTERTAINMENT

My values and morals in life didn't add up to this lifestyle from the beginning, but I got myself into the situation and also wanted to experience, which I feel is a great experience for every young girl to experience once at least to see if it's something that she feels she can have fun in this way—expressing herself in her birthday suit. Also if she feels she could learn valuable lessons and get ahead in life faster than working a nine-to-five or going to school for four years, this could pay for school for four years.

It really truly helped me become a woman learning the power behind being a woman. I learned new ways to do my makeup. I learned new ways to dance. I learned how to become a seducer, a flirt, a hustler, a tease. I learned the value of money because I had a lot of it. I learned my boundaries. I learned my time was money and I was worth a lot of it. I was the Creator of my Reality. I was in control of my life. It was all a lie to the people I loved. Nobody knew, only my one friend until one day one of my husband's friends walked in and saw me waiting to go on stage and he left.

But called me that night and told me I needed to go and tell my husband before he did and I did but at that time I did not confess about having sex with my first love. I only confessed about stripping. It was a month before he got out. He had some time to think about it. So he came home from prison; I quit stripping and got a job as a caregiver, which I loved. I was making only $9.00 an hour. In the year 2000, I was twenty-one years old. We had our little apartment. My car was fixed because of all the money from stripping. He had a new wardrobe when he got out, a new gold chain. Things were good until my cocaine addiction from stripping continued and I got caught. I got manipulated into telling the truth about my first love and I having sex one time while he was locked up.

That day was the day me and my first husband broke up. It didn't matter. Everything I had done for him, all the visits, everything that I stressed about and experienced because of our relationship. Me having to keep an apartment so he had somewhere to parole to, none of it mattered. He said that if I would've told the truth when I confessed about the stripping about that situation sleeping with my ex one time in thirteen months; I slept with one person, and then he would've been able to think about it like he did the stripping situation for a month and he would've been able to forgive me but because it happened after him getting out, his excuse was he couldn't forgive me. I lost my job as a caregiver because I kept crying and I couldn't care for anybody. I couldn't even care for myself. I didn't love myself. I had a broken heart.

So I went on a vacation to visit my family in California to get away. I was brokenhearted. My first broken heart, it was tragic. I never thought anybody had felt the way I felt at that time. (I was the only one that felt that much pain in the world.) How dramatic of me, huh? I laugh about it now! My broken heart, it was intense. While I was there on vacation, I got a call from my roommate. She had not come up with her part of the rent. I only needed $400. I didn't have my dancing clothes with me. Let me tell you, I never asked my family for money ever. I was embarrassed that I had spent all the money on my husband that I had gotten when I turned eighteen from being run over at two years old. You can say he was kind of a gigolo.

I was very kind, giving young lady and he saw that I was naïve. So, I was taking full responsibility for myself always, never reaching out for help. So I got creative ideas constantly. I also learned later in life that I act better in moments of chaos. It's kind of why I always have a lot going on around me. I act better when I create a little chaos than it being peaceful and quiet around me when I was younger. Today I value peace and quiet when I'm creating so I can meditate and have inspired action only in my life guided by my higher intelligence instead of acting purely from my ego self. Escorting, call girl, privates, dating continuing from the call I received from my roommate. I got an idea to look in the phonebook and I found a few escorting services and only got one that was taking new girls at that time. I told him my situation that I used to strip in a club in Eugene, Oregon and I was on vacation and I needed the money for rent. he said come on over, so I headed to Riverside, California.

My first call was in Big Bear across the street from Heather Locklear's house. I remember I made $700 in one hour. At that point stripping was chump change, in comparison to being a call girl but now the danger of something bad happening was higher. I never went without a driver, which is what I called them—aka soldier boys—because they were always strapped up and down for the cause. Now anybody that is considering this lifestyle, I'm going to tell you this and I cannot stress it enough. The number one thing is safety. Always safety first when proceeding in this industry in person. I was so scared I remember asking the owner of the agency so what exactly was I supposed to do? He said only what you're comfortable doing. He said it's a regular client of his, so I will be safe.

He told me you were a stripper before. Do the same dance that you used to do on the stage for him in private and that's exactly what I did. I just did a striptease the man asked if he could play with himself while I did my exotic dance and that was the worst that I had ever had to experience during the calls. But once you've seen one "D," you've seen them all. In my mind at least it wasn't touching me and I wasn't required to touch it because when I go on normal dates, I don't go and touch a guy's dick or allow him to even show me it or touch his self on a first date. That's not what I would do, so why would I do that being paid for it? Values, morals standards, boundaries—this is what I took with me to the streets of such a dangerous game. This is what made it to where I felt empowered when I looked in the mirror, when I was home and safe at night and knowing that I could get in and out and have clients satisfied without any complaints or any physical sexual gratification from me other than the live fantasies I provided.

I'll give a list of fantasies and fetishes that I provided later in this chapter. I would power trip on that. I made my rent money and a little more for Christmas presents and ended my trip. So, I flew back to Oregon and I had a four-hour layover in Portland, which is two hours north of Eugene and called a close friend to come visit me because I was in his town. So, he came to me right away. Well, I asked him for some cocaine after I told him what I had just experienced in California. He introduced me to crystal meth. I was twenty-one years old at this time. The friend said that it was better to do because you needed less of it and it lasted longer. I changed my flight that day. We went straight to the strip clubs.

In Portland they had a magazine in every strip club. My friend told me about it so we picked one up. It was for escorts. It was an adult entertainer magazine called *Exotica*. It was a magazine where the dancers and escorts would advertise themselves and companies. Life was going so fast that literally I was so young and dumb and thirsty for experience and for money. So, I met a big-time escort named Lexy. She had her own service She's what I liked to call an independent woman. She was known in the industry by lots of people. Her clients were thousand-dollar clients. Half of her clients were cops and married men. One thing was they were all regulars.

She did get new guys too, but the ones she sent me to were her regulars; the ones she trained me with were her regulars, which means they were safe. They weren't guys that were going to cause any problems. She would build relationships, long-term relationships with these men. See, let me describe Lexy to you: blonde, tan, fake boobs, model body, lived with her ex-boyfriend, had her own room, cute room. She loved to tan and spray tan every day. I forget the car; she had put on the bumper of her car a sticker and it said *I love to tweak* and she was addicted to crystal meth as well. She taught me how to live on the drug and not get all not functioning. She was what I call a veteran tweaker. She was all about business. She would wear wigs on her calls because Lexy was balding, probably because the drugs were causing psoriasis on her head.

So she needed girls like me to team up with her to help keep her clients happy with fresh faces. She took me under her wing and she trained me. I learned everything from her about this game. I was quiet back then. I was good at observing. I paid close attention to every move she made. I learned how to take calls and that was where the magic was because anybody can take out ads and market something, but if you can't make those calls go through, it was all a waste of money. I learned from the best. Ninety percent of the calls that came in, if she didn't make them go through, I did. Life was going so fast. I was there with her for about a month maybe less and then I went back to Eugene, Oregon with the money I had made. I promised to come back every weekend.

QUICK GUIDE/PRIVATE CALLS/DATING

#1) SAFETY FIRST. Never ever be alone. Always have someone with you that you can count on. I used to call them my (soldiers) because you want a down-ass person and I say person because you can have a female or male, someone you know no matter what will have your back and can get you out safely. This is for the soldier boys, job details, or soldier girl have a safety code they have to always know what room you are in and be watching for a light to flicker, and if that light flickers, they have to be ready to bust down the door or jump through a window I've never had to do this because, first you're going to call and check in and let them know that you got the $200 for the hour already put away hidden somewhere and that you feel safe. If you don't feel safe you need a code word to let them know you're not feeling safe, which would mean they need to come in and get you right then.

So you always have that moment if you get the money first, which that is number two but #1 is safety. The date needs to know someone knows where you are. They don't really need to know that they're there with you sometimes that freaks them out to think someone's outside. Just try to be short when they ask questions about that. Just be clear that you, for safety reasons, let someone know when you arrive somewhere and that you feel safe out of protection for yourself so the person you're visiting knows that you're not dumb and that you're not there and nobody knows where you are. You can even take it a step further and let them know that someone has your location if you don't want them to know that someone is outside. Try to be cute and sexy and always speak to them in a nonthreatening voice, soft and giggle a lot.

#2) ALWAYS MONEY FIRST/LIST OF LIVE FANTASIES right when you get there all negotiations should be done either prior to arriving or right when you arrive and you feel the room out and the person and see if you're comfortable. About $200 an hour is a going rate for most common cities. In a big city, a going rate is a $1000 an hour for full service, and $2000 an hour for full service from an escort who is considered a porn star. Other than that, the normal going rate is $1000 an hour for a full service in big cities. Full service is only after three dates. I'm gonna say this a lot to get you to remember: (you do not want a prostitution charge) you're just trying to get ahead and play a sexy fun profitable game that can be a good way to pay for things you desire in life. Continuing what I was saying, the reason you want all negotiations done at the beginning is because you don't want to be already undressed and then making negotiations. It's not safe. They have to at the very beginning already know what they're going to be getting.

You can say things like: "I like to get it out of the way. How much fun are we going to have?" "Discuss with me what your fantasies are?" "This is the list of what I provide.") It's better to do on the phone prior, but if all of a sudden, they see you are who you say you are and they want more, you can list these fantasies for them, but they all cost extra. (Never say you will have sex with them. Never say you won't.) You can say anything in a baby, sexy cute voice with a man and especially if you're already naked and get what you want, which is to get in and out of there without having sex for money because you do not want to get a prostitution charge. This is called dating for a reason.

You need three dates with someone who is paying for your time for it to NOT be a prostitution charge. You can let the customer know they need to see you (three times) before they ever ask you that question. Whether you're going to have sex or not, you need a relationship with them. You need to know they are not a cop. A cop will not see you three times unless they're dating you. I HAVE HAD CALLS WITH COP CLIENTS AND UNDER-COVER COPS, AND I PROMISE YOU THIS IS THE LAW. I had a probation officer tell me once it is not illegal to sell girls. It's illegal to sell drugs. I've NEVER GOTTEN A prostitution charge.

Striptease, sexy dancing, and lap dancing are part of the call, so are sensual rubdowns. Those are natural things that go with the $200 for the hour. Live fantasies are but not limited to also $100 extra for each one is reasonable, but you can choose what you're willing to provide and comfortable with and what it's worth to you for the extras (shower shows, toy shows, foot fetish shows, role-play, tickle shows, or light S&M or just a party with me call or dinner or I just want to talk or hug calls), also bachelor parties for ten people and up are $500 plus tips, twenty people is $1000 and it doesn't matter if they tip; only get one hour or it's another hour of pay.

#3) THE FOUR NOS:

1. NO CUTE GUYS

2. NO YOUNG GUYS

3. NO CHEAP GUYS

4. NO HIGH OR DRUNK GUYS

The reason no to all of these is (what they have in common) they are all trying to get something for nothing. The cute guys think because they're cute, they can get a discount once you get there and it's harder to tell them NO; the young guys the same thing, and they really don't have the money for your time nine times out of ten; the cheap guys on the phone I used to say a certain race was showing me their cheapness, but I realized it doesn't matter what the race is. You can tell on the phone when a guy is being cheap when they're belittling the price of $200 for the hour when you know you're high quality. If they don't just take your word for it and you have to waste your breath too much, they are not worth your time. I don't care. It will not be a safe situation. They will try to get something for nothing if they're showing on the phone that they're being cheap. The high guys, if they want to play with themselves they won't be successful without help from you, so it's better to not have a regular call routine like strip dance and rubdowns with them.

I'm not saying don't go on a call where someone's partying, but don't ever except any drugs from them. Bring your own. Don't ever let them open a drink for you. You do it yourself and don't let your drink out of your sight and don't get naked in front of them because you won't be able to have a regular call with them because they will be intoxicated. They won't be able to satisfy themselves, so it will make your job harder and unsafe. That's why these are all "no" rules, because anytime I ignored one of these rules, I regretted it, which is only a handful of times out of the years I jumped in and out of this game. Another thing I forgot to mention: never say you do massages because you're not a licensed masseuse. It's better to say sensual rubdowns. You can get arrested for saying massage when you're not a licensed massage therapist. It's a sensual rubdown.

#4) The three date rule. Let's say after three dates, you don't want to have sex with that person, you've gotten to know them. You know they're not a cop. You trust them. They have become a regular client now, so you can always go on a fourth date and bring a girl and say that you have to train her. Tell him that you will give him a two for one special so they only have to pay one price—$200 for the hour—for both of you, but if they want to have full fun with the two of you, then you charge the $1000 but bring a girl with you who is willing to have sex with the guy. A girl who already has sex with all the guys she goes on regular dates with anyway. She has to know and agree to this. And if you know that this guy is not a cop, it will be okay to bring the girl with you on the fourth date or you can also say I have to treat us like the first date with you on the fourth date because I'm training this girl by the fifth date you can send a girl by herself or you could go with for the $1000 for the hour only after you've built trust and had three paid dates with that guy yourself.

#5) Make the girls sign independent contracts, You can pick them up at Office Depot or Office-Max. An office supply store will have independent contracts for the models/exotic dancers/girls that work for you or with you. It's for your protection legally as well. I've never needed this. It's just to be cautious and more professional because you can pay taxes on something like those if you were in the phonebook and you kept all your receipts or if you used a square and it gets direct deposited somehow with a cash app or PayPal. You could actually take a credit card as well on your phone goes directly to your account. That's one way to keep track of the money coming in or you could also just get cash the old-fashioned way.

#6) MONEY/SPLIT always pay your girl that is working with you right away. Give her half of whatever you make at the date. While there, get the money out of the way RIGHT AWAY, AFTER YOU GET PAID. With your girl you have with you your teammate, your independent contractor, exotic entertainer money always gets handled first in all directions. After the call, you pay your driver 10% of whatever your earnings are. You get that out of the way right away in this business. If everybody is making money and everybody is happy, there will be no drama. It's when somebody feels like they didn't get their cut or they feel scammed that things will go bad. I have seen it happen with other agencies but never with mine or never to me, but it does happen you follow this rule everybody needs to be making money or there could be drama.

#7) SOLDIER/DRIVER/ BOY/OR GIRL RULES They get 10%. They are aware of this when they get hired. The rules are they are not to be seen or heard ever. You call and check in with them to let them know you got the money and that you're safe with a code word. They can come and get you only to be seen if you are in trouble; not before, not ever before unless it's for a bachelor party. Bachelor parties are to be seen and not heard, and they need to look scary. If they are conversing with people, that makes them not scary. Quiet people are scary. You don't know what to expect. They are to stay quiet and look intimidating the whole time. They do not collect the money for you. They are not your pimp. You always collect your money and hold your money. They are not responsible. You should always know where your money is at all times. Their job is to protect you and to be on point, not conversing and hanging out with anybody. Always eyes are on you and near you at all times.

Now we're not on calls. If you do not have a car, your driver is required to take you to get your hair, your nails, your outfits, maybe you're living out of hotels, to take you to and from hotel rooms—a driver to me is a true pimp. How pimps should be protecting and taking you places and providing security so you can do your thing and hustle on in safe environments knowing that they are there for protection. That is what it should be about. I have no respect for pimps in the old-day world of this industry. They have a bad name, a bad reputation, but to me, if a driver sticks with these rules, they actually deserve more than 10%. I've really paid my drivers in the past. I take care of them and they take care of me. I was making car payments for them, house payments for them, and I was always taken care of and I never was without a driver's protection… ever. Priorities, ladies, priorities.

SUGAR BABIES

Okay so if you are not into stripping for dollars at all but would like to be a sugar baby, let me tell you the difference between a sugar daddy or being a sugar baby. A sugar daddy gets sex and intimacy all the time; as a sugar baby, you don't have sex. There's a financial agreement of some kind made at the beginning, so it is not ever a question about what part each plays in each other's life. Consider them a sponsor, a guide, or a dad you never had. The amount of money is discussed right away and time that is to be spent together is discussed. All at the beginning of the relationship, goals and dreams are discussed and respected from both sides. I have been a sugar baby for nineteen years with one man he is heaven-sent. I love and respect him 100%.

I found out from a past life that he used to be my brother and I took care of him, so in this life-time he's indebted to me to make me successful, to teach me a lot of valuable lessons about myself my personality and my goals to becoming successful on my own. That is the only thing that has ever made sense to me ever, and I just now discovered that after nineteen years of him being there for me, the only stable thing in my life financially and my best friend and I coparent with him both my children. It's an unbelievable situation. No sugar baby situation will be the same, but with these guidelines, it could help you to make it the best experience for you that it possible. Could be this is a good stepping-stone towards a good life that you could create being a sugar baby. It's a very good opportunity. It's a rare woman that can use this experience to her advantage and it be a positive in her life. A real diamond in my eyes.

So being a sugar baby, you want to value his work ethics, needs, whatever they may be. You go over it with him at the very beginning. How often he would like to see you, but figure it all out at the beginning because this shows him you're of service to him not just a pretty face. So you add to his life and not just take. So, find out by asking questions about his life and his routines. What's missing in his life? Then you do the same. You volunteer information if he doesn't ask about what's missing in your life, especially your financial situation and your dreams and goals that cost money. If you don't like the way you are living, express that to him but also give him input of where you would like to live. It really could be a number of things so I really couldn't list all of them, but I will list a few so you can get an idea of a very professional man's life you may need to travel with him. He may need a traveling buddy for different reasons, business or pleasure trips or he doesn't like eating alone, so dinners, maybe even church; you get it.

There may be different types of social events or occasion so you would also need to dress for the situation presentably and be a great actress but sincere. You will be building a solid relationship with him, so be honest about your needs as well really know what you want and need and total amounts for things. Really look into what you want and know the cost before you go into a conversation about money or goals or dreams and always listen closely and repeat what you hear. It's called good listening skills. Don't go and try to be a sugar baby if you don't have any class. Stick with stripping or parties or escorting or adult porn. You will be letting yourself feel like a failure if you try to level up and you're not mature enough or have proper etiquette. So really know yourself and your abilities to be a good sugar baby.

Okay so another thing if you are or want to be a sugar baby you will need to check in daily. Don't always wait for a busy man to contact you. Consider this your job now to care about his day, not always just to call for money. Make him your best friend. You can always count on. You know, like the dad you never had. I know my dad wasn't there like I needed him to be. I also felt he could've done a lot better providing for my needs and wants and love and support then he actually dif. So now you know how to look at the situation you are getting into and why you're fulfilling needs that were never met. I have shared this with men I've dated with advice for how to take care of their daughters or their daughters will end up like me and many other gorgeous girls trying to become women too fast. This is the fast way to discover how to use your woman power and how to stay in control of your situation of not having a good father to teach you how to be treated by men. You may need to go to movies with him; you may need to go shopping with him. Allow him to know your life of likes and dislikes with food and clothes and interests. Maybe you want to go further your education and you need a sponsor to pay for your school or you wish to start a business. Be smart about your every move and conversation.

You have be open to sharing your bills, amount of debt worries, all of the above. Don't be shy or whiny about it. Be considerate and always show gratitude for every little thing that is done for you. A ballpark price on time is $200 an hour, but if you have an agreement for all your bills and spending cash paid in full at the first of the month; then it's your job to keep up with your part daily to prove your worth helping, that you're a good added bonus to his life. You need equal give-and-take. No matter what, karma needs you to give to get, so be of service. I helped build his home because he didn't have the time to go to all the appointments. He was building a home. I had to pick out everything with the builders of his home.

That's an example of how to help out. It took me a year to build his home for him all the way down to putting the furniture inside of it. If he would have hired someone else to do that, it could've cost thousands and thousands. Better it be me and then it had my magical touch on it. Also, I got the experience added to my references. I could be an interior decorator if I wanted because I got that experience. You get to feel what's missing in such a wonderful man's life. Learn new things, take lessons, grow into the lady that you wish to become with no money worries. Treat this like the best opportunity you could ever have had. He needs to feel valued. There has to be an equal give-and-take between the two of you for it to work long-term and that's with anything you do in life regarding relationships especially. You will love him, for sure, and you never know; maybe you will fall in love with him but never have sex with him before you get married because of the situation with the money agreement. Make sure he just isn't challenged because you never have had sex. Some very intelligent men are very competitive and so make sure it's really love if you decide to be traditional about it.

SUGAR DADDY

You wanna make sure that you build a relationship first so the three-or-more-date rule is important and establishing a relationship first before any sexual encounters are to happen with a sugar daddy. In the quick guide rules, you want to follow and building a relationship needs to be established before the sex part is introduced to the relationship. I can't say this enough, very important when having a sugar daddy is to stay in full control of you. Your personal power needs to constantly be acknowledged. You say who, you say where, and you say when. It's a power trip on your part but done with respect. The only real difference is there's sex involved in some way with a sugar daddy relationship; there is no sex involved with being a sugar baby like I said in the last chapter.

If not just sex, a lot of intimacy is involved. So you do all the same things like have an amount hourly for sure, but make sure you keep your boundaries. You don't really need to spend so much time, though, because there is more you're giving of your personal power and your body so you have to make sure there is respect on both sides of time and space. $200 an hour is the minimum but you can also set a monthly price, but then you will have to add in some of the things that sugar babies do as well, so that will complicate things. It's kind of better to stick with an hourly rate when you're giving your body to someone for money and having a situation where you're spoiled. Know your boundaries and stick to them. Don't change them continuously. Be consistent. If you don't want him to see you without makeup, then don't let him see you without makeup.

If he wants to bring you something to your place, you have him leave it at the door. Some sugar-baby situations start out like sugar-daddy situations, but they never lead into sex because of one reason or another the man can't perform or whatever because of age; then it will become a sugar-baby situation, but you won't know until you communicate openly with your new financial friend. In big city areas or expensive living areas and communities you could charge $1000 an hour for full-service relationships. You decide if it's a high-quality man or not by his car his watch, clothes, shoes, grooming, his home if you see it with your own eyes. You should know who you're dealing with and who he is. Google him or do a people search to make sure he is who he says he is. Look up his company before any sexual relations are involved and always get the money up front. Just have an agreement from the beginning when your time starts unless you felt trust and you know he'll pay you afterwards.

Ask a lot of questions. Play detective. You know it's the same as if you, me, a man, and you are just dating him you want to know who you have in your presence. Don't make it be any different just because you're receiving money from him. Social media finds out if he's married by asking him and then also on a people search. You could find out make sure there's no crazy exes involved or other adult entertainers that are pissed off at him. Have morals, have values, and boundaries I can't say this enough. It's called self-respect. Take care of yourself. Do not allow him to control you, and when you see each other or talk or text because you need to be in control of your time and your body at all times. I call it "pussy power." Control your pussy or someone else will.

I know it's vulgar to say it like this. I'm sorry. I'm just keeping it real. This life isn't for everybody but sometimes being a woman, you have to do what you have to do. Just be honest and sincere and have fun life. Life is supposed to be fun. Do you remember as a child ever wanting to go anywhere if it wasn't going to be fun? Why does it have to be any different? Just because we're adults, it doesn't make sure you're having fun at all times in your life. Enjoy your life. Don't just live; build a life you enjoy. I don't agree with a man being dominant over a woman ever. This experience should help you learn how to speak up for yourself and how to be in control in a man's world. It should teach you the power a woman has and how to use it to climb to the top of any field or accomplish any dream you have no matter what. Always speak in a sexy sweet voice, even when you don't want to. You can say anything you want as long as you stay in a sweet sexy character always. You will be able to get a message across to a man clearly no matter how mean and direct you're being as long as you stay sexy and in a sweet voice with the deliverance being respectful. That's a "no matter what" with any of these adult world hustling situations you're doing.

Stripping, dating, AK escorting, sugar baby, sugar daddy—it doesn't matter. It will work every time to get your message or a request heard. If you make sure you stay sweet and sexy with your voice. Practice it if you must. That is gold information there, but for me I did have a hard time after a few years being a sugar baby because I was not a nice person. I was high on something most of the time or coming down, but when I wasn't, I was mean, really mean. So really be aware of your situation and do a lot of self-reflection if you want it to last. I did do that and when you're growing right before your financial friend's eyes, it's a good thing as well because they helped make you who you are today. I know from nineteen years' experience that if it wasn't for his love and wisdom and respect and financial support, I wouldn't be here writing this book today.

He is such a wonderful man inside and out. He knows how to make money like the rest of them, but he was raised different and that's a good and bad thing, but all financially successful men who would reach out to a professional sex worker or call girl, exotic entertainer, porn star, escort have in common is they want a sexy woman by their side—but only when they want one. Perhaps they are so busy and have had so many either failed marriages or they fear commitment or really just don't value a real relationship, so getting a pro to spend some free time with for whatever the reason—dinner, sensual rubdown, events, traveling, and holidays whatever the occasion—they really value freedom over all the work it takes to make it work with a nice girl they could take home to Mom. So a pro is best in the rise and more fun, which is usually lacking in their lives, so why not? I don't judge and you shouldn't either because any girl that's doing this for a living and loving it, really is the same and values her freedom just like that very successful man.

We as women just wanna have fun as well. You just need to always remember to invest right away, though, because fast money goes fast, so always have a plan or you will lose it somehow or have to spend it quick on something because of the spiritual laws, the law of cause-and-effect. I will get into that soon. So that's finishing up sugar daddy's. Also, one more thing: you don't need to involve your family life with them. I don't recommend it. I do for sugar baby situations, but not for the sugar daddy situations. It's not necessary. Use your own GPS intuition system we have built into our bodies to decide if you want to involve them with your family, but a sugar daddy, I would not involve with my family. The reason is it causes complications in the family because of the money and you not marrying him them, judging and attachments and it's no one's business. Okay, one more thing, make sure any gifts that are given are in your name because it's not yours unless it's in your name.

DADS HOW TO NOT

I was a daddy's girl I was told by my mom that my-dad worked two jobs, He was a really good provider. I love my dad very much. This isn't a dad bashing situation. Okay, guys, little girls need to feel special. They need to learn how to love a man by watching moms love their dad and they learn how to be loved by men by how much love is received from Dad and how Mom is showing love from Dad. Anything that is not healthy, yes, will have an effect on your daughters and your sons, but we're talking about daughters right now. Your daughter is judgment later in life. We also have to know some astrology signs are just more wild in nature. Let's say, like my family, they don't know how strong character flaws can make a difference. Financially your daughter needs to feel you are her rock, her knight in shining armor, and that she can always, no matter what, always count on you.

So at a young age, always show her that by not discussing money worries or debts with her. Kids in general do not need to know about finances, money struggles at a young age. I'm sure it's a sign of abuse somewhere. Also, no matter what, always show up to whatever she is involved in and no matter what, you need to be your daughter's biggest fan with everything she does in life. You should always ask her if she has money or just slip her some if you know she will not ask for it. Go on dates with her; no age is too early and no age is too late to start taking your daughter on a private date with you so you can talk and get to know her. Also, so she can get to know you as well outside of the home and away from others. Be really involved in her relationships with her friends and boys and teachers. Give her freedom to go where and be who she wants to be but have your say as well.

Always show her love and verbally tell her you love her frequently. If she gets into trouble, you need to be the one she wants to call first and, no matter what, you show up. No matter what. Never ever, ever, ever break a promise. Never hit your baby girl no matter what age she is. If she needs a cosigner for anything, always sign for her and support her if she has no place to live. No matter what, you always welcome her into your home. Never let any woman even her mom come between you. Always have your daughter's back. Be honest with her. Be at her wedding even if there are several of them. Be a good grandpa. Be involved in the kids' life but always be her go-to for someone to talk to.

KELLY KEITH

Don't ever push her away. If you have the money, spoil her, but time is really most important. Emotional support from a father doesn't cost anything. Just determination to not have a daughter that goes for the wrong attention for the wrong reasons or because she needs to because she has no one to turn to. Or because she is looking for a father she never had period. Period.

HOW TO MARKET/ ADVERTISE YOURSELF

Okay so you're gonna wanna take really pleasing to the eye sexy pictures and you're going to need ID because half of these places online now want to verify you are who you say you are so they know for sure you're not being trafficked or you're not being forced against your will. This is today's world in the industry, which I think is very smart. I agree with the way they're doing it now.

any free area local newspapers

Yellow phonebook online

Business cards

Website/linktree.com

sexyjobs.com

YouTube

privatedelights.com

Euro Instagram subscription

Snapchat subscription only

fans.com

local adult magazines   usually find them in strip clubs or porn stores, mainstream, work, weekly newspapers, etc., you just have to be low-key about your advertising misstravel.com

seekingarrangements.com

golddiggers.com

establishgentleman.com

livejasmin.com

Webcam porn

Phone sex operator

Google it; there's so many listed

Portland Oregon has exotica magazine

sugardaddy's site.org

ASTROLOGY

So, I have been self-educating for twenty-two years and counting now using and learning all different ways to use astrology in my life as a helpful tool. People who say it's not true, are uneducated; don't ever try to convince a skeptic ever, ever, ever. Number one rule: don't waste your breath trying to convince anybody that astrology is real. It's science. It's facts. I started on web TV. I never thought I would like the internet until I found astrology on Astrocenter.com. The site is huge now, but it was only a single page back then but very accurate, very detailed, very clear, and very on point with describing who I was and putting it into words for myself to learn how to describe who I was to people.

I was twenty-one years old I was going through a separation with my first husband and I was brokenhearted. I was running full speed ahead in my life at the time, and not wanting to slow down because my heart hurt so bad. Well, I started reading my husband's personality first. He was a Pisces. I was trying to understand where I went wrong. I felt I needed to learn his personality, and maybe I could save my marriage if I could just understand who he was. So, after I read about him, I started to read about myself; then I read about us together, our compatibility. I was a reading machine. So, we did get back together, but I learned that when there are too many scars on the relationship, it's too far past saving. I did learn a new tool, though, to use because of the pain, so that was a plus. Well, I'm finding out now it was part of my destiny anyway.

Well, I used to go to church, but for six weeks in a row in Eugene, Oregon, I wasn't getting a message at church because the church was only discussing how they needed money every Sunday for six weeks in a row. I needed something more, so I went off to the bookstore. I went to the New Age section, which had grown tremendously over the years. It's called the new age section at the bookstore. I started my book collection and studied nonstop while I was abusing drugs the whole time.

I have a reason for saying that, and I'll come back to it in a minute.

I study numerology and Chinese astrology colors. I was avoiding Tarot, of course, because I thought it was the devil because I still thought I was Christian. Just a hypocritical one; anyways, not true. I found a tarot deck that was planet, suns, moon, stars, and astrology, so it wasn't the traditional deck of cards. I got comfortable with that; then I moved on to a more really advanced deck. The intuitive Tarot. It didn't have a lot of details on it. I really had to use my gut instincts and build my intuition with that deck. It was the best deck, I would say, from my first stack, knowing who I am today in a past life I already was an advanced tarot reader. I learned that the reason I learned in that order—astrology, numerology, Chinese astrology, colors, and then the tarot—was not by accident but from a past life regression. I found out that in my past lives, I knew all of those things very well and I knew that that was the order to learn it and subconsciously.

We all have the "clair" abilities clairvoyance, clairaudience, clairsentience, and claircognizance, but there's always one that stands out more. Mine is claircognizance; that's inner knowing. Learning in that order helped me to be a more accurate tarot reader, and all of those things help assist being a tarot reader and having the knowledge in all those categories of Divination tools. So now I'm twenty-three years old. Been using Divination in my life for a couple years, and I was a natural. I loved it. I studied the planets next on the astronomical union's website, went straight to the source. I had some books as well. I'll mention later with another chapter of tech I used. I learned about Neptune's energy and we had been stuck on a merry-go-round for 2000 years. Neptune's energy represents dreams, illusions, addictions, nightmares, artists, writers, and things that keep you in your mind and on a kind of repeat over and over again. I don't like merry-go-rounds, I used to say.

If you tried to do a 180 degree turn around and change your life, you could only get a few feet ahead of your game but then keep going in circles. Okay, let me get to the point. I learned while you are in your addictions, you are taking your hardhat off of identity to figure out who you really are under the mask. You were playing every day, so while you're high you will have repeating behavior that will be noticeable to others around you and yourself and you are supposed to learn who you are through the addiction by finding a workable talent that maybe you wouldn't have seen if you were not high doing it over and over excessively let me tell you my things for an example so maybe this could help you discover yours and my talents were makeup.

I loved it. I did it over and over. I took it off. I put it back on a few times in a day to learn new ways of putting it on and blending. I became a certified media makeup artist and body painter. Anything new age I was into and I was talented at it and I would give readings to my friends and predictions or clients while I was painting them. Photography I'm really good at taking sexy pictures it's so easy for me to make a woman look sexually desirable in a picture. I also was trying to be a life coach back then but I didn't know what it was called I was trying to do a homemaker turn supermodel makeover I even got the girl a boob lift because she had a bad boob job and I was trying to "mind, body, soul extreme makeover" on her. I was really finding myself through my addiction; it helped me become who I am today. The addiction loses its power when you find a workable talent within the addiction. I found out I'm the mental accomplishment card in the deck of cards. It's the 10 of clubs. Which means I will be trying to find the right occupation most of my life, to find my purpose, and I did do just that.

Everything happens for a reason. Your whole life is mapped out for you. I will get more into that in the last chapter, but I want to discuss how I was kind of mad about that when I first started studying astrology and I did take a lot of breaks from it throughout the years, but I always did tarot readings for close people or friends, family, and people I felt called to do so. I did use astrology before hiring people to see if we would get along or if they would be good for the job. I used it in all my relationships. I studied my kids just a few years ago, though, and family members. One of my kids is my karma cousin, which makes sense why people thought he was my favorite. He was a mini version of myself and my other son is my past life card. So crazy. All my exes were no mediocre relationships. They all played a part in my growth and I learned this all through astrology. I can help you as well if you would like. I would love to be a part of your journey as well. Also, location astrology is the best thing to help you discover where to live and to buy a house or just to visit to help you grow into the person at different stages in your life just in your environment. Knowing which location line to be on can help you advance and grow and mature so much faster than waiting for life to happen to you.

Actually being the creator of your reality, everyday astrology is meant to be used in your life every day. I never used to use it every day, and if I did, I would read about today's astrology, but I never read about tomorrow's to get a head start. And you're supposed to start your day with your astrology reading not read it at the end of the day.

KELLY KEITH

I was doing it all backwards or used to do moon rit-
uals wishes during the full moon, and you're supposed to do that during the new moon for many
years up until three years ago, I was doing things
backwards because I jumped in and out of it too
many years in a row because I was intoxicated on
something all the time, but I've been sober now for
almost 3 years and counting and staying this way;
and I'm learning so fast how to create my reality
and how to manifest. So simple to live the life of
your dreams. It's amazing to me that this was all
here before and I'm just now seeing it.

TRUSTED SPIRITUAL BOOKS/TECH USED

It makes sense because the truth is coming out with this new world we live in because of Aquarius times. Aquarius energy is about growth and love and truth, logically speaking, expansion. Not being on a merry-go-round bettering yourself every day, enjoying your life only doing things that you enjoy. You can even follow Astrology for finances. JP Morgan Chase says billionaires follow Astrology not millionaires. What do you want to be? The sky is the limit. Make this lifetime the best one. These are the best of days to be having a human experience. You are the creator of your reality. No one is to blame for where you are right now. If you don't like where you are, you can change it right now right now right now.

All you have to do is get tuned in, tapped in, and turned on:

astrocenter.com

align 27 app

The biorhythm map

numerologist.com

Gaia TV app

Achieve today app

Yoda pro app

Pattern app

YouTube

tarot readers café

astrology.com

free natal chart quizzes

lonerwolf.com

BOOKS:

Linda Goodman love signs

Destiny cards by Robert Lee Camp

Love Cards by Robert Lee Camp

Think and Grow Rich by Napoleon Hill

Ask and It Is Given Esther and Jerry Hicks

Intuitive Astrology bye Elizabeth rose Camp-
bell

The Secret Language of Birthdays by Gary
Goldschneider and Joost Elffers

Sylvia Brown's book

The secret language of Destiny by Gary
Goldschneider and Joost Elffers

Animal Speaks by Andrews

Finding Your True North Star by Martha
Beck Pendulum Magic by Richard Webster

The Secret Language of Relationships by
Gary Goldschneider and Joost Elffers

Soul consciousness by Karen Dever

Crystal Bible by Judy Hall

The secret universe of names by Roy Feinson

How psychic are you? By Paul Roland

PURPOSE/DESTINY

I said a few chapters back that I didn't like astrology when I was young, so I took breaks from it and tried to only use it for entertainment purposes. The reason for this was because I didn't like how our lives were destined to be in the future to turn out the same. Well, let me explain more about how purpose works.

Well, soul maps we are supposed to start studying our sign first. Then work it into our lives by studying others but how they relate to ourselves, and then you will start to see patterns like small or big groups of people of the same sign and train your inner circle at different times in your life. They rotate clockwise every few months. You will find it kind of strange that all your exes were a certain sign or your friends are the same or whatever the reason is you are meant to take something from each sign and learn from their personality what you like in yourself or what you end up finding out.

They could be past lives with unfinished soul contracts needing to be completed, but really we have twelve signs, some double, some triple, in each sign that represent different parts of our personality. So you are not just one sign or three; you are sun moon rising. You're actually twelve and planets that rule those signs affect our personality all of it in different ways good and bad. So well… there's no real good or bad. I would just say positive and negative strengths and weaknesses in our personalities really because there really is no good or bad in life. I'll explain that later. So, the easier way to learn instead of years like I did is to go to caféastrology.com click on free natal charts and learn all your signs and meanings and then learn how the planets affect you. That website really helps you and it's free and it helps you understand it so easy and puts it into words for you to be able to describe yourself to people.

So you could discover your perfect self. We are all trying to be perfect. We are all trying to better ourselves to be the godly sides of ourselves. We have sources energy in all of us. Being connected to source through meditation makes a mind-body-soul connection. There are personality traits in every sign of the zodiac that we should take into our own personality to better ourselves and become a part of every sign to have higher consciousness god-like minds. To better understand people from knowing the zodiac strengths and weaknesses of every sign so you can become one consciousness and accept everyone because you understand everyone to be in a mindful state of being one mind understanding people even without words. having compassion for the next person. All of us working at being better people it's just understanding each other more on a deeper level so we can start learning unconditional love by truly understanding people and accepting people for who they are or are trying to be. We need to all be raising our vibration to better ourselves, no matter what right now.

There are good parts of all the zodiac signs and that is what we are a little bit of each of those all into one being, which is the meaning. We are all one consciousness because we are all going to better ourselves no matter what. It's the winning side of this game, the matrix we chose to come and play, and yes we have free will, but there are twelve universal laws and rules to follow and astrology is just an introduction. I will go over the laws from my perception in a simple version in the last chapter. If you study yourself seriously, you will find your purpose is hidden in your personality and when I say purpose I mean the American dream, finding what you love and making a living doing what you're passionate about and also what you came to complete from other lives.

Life really could be fun every day if you know who you are. These are the answers to the questions: Who are you? Where are you going? How do you show emotion? How can you serve? What's most important to you? These questions will change your life if you know the answers to them. Honestly, these questions can guide you to your purpose and always remember the only thing that is constant is change. So, you will never stop learning my mantra is learning to love and loving to learn!

SLOW BOAT TO CHINA

This is a metaphor that I have found myself asking people since I discovered that I was doing this the hard way. After getting sober and surrendering to my higher self to source energy or bouncing in and out of my addiction, I would ask would you rather take a slow boat to China or the jet? I was in total awareness that I was taking the harder road in life.

Now think about it a slow boat to China, hypothetically speaking, a person could go through a lot of trials and traumas near life death experiences slowly learning while learning about so much contrast but not getting to the destination for years decades it would feel obstacle after obstacle a lot of darkness, and not seen the light at the end of the tunnel Or would you rather take a jet? Still headed the same direction but actually have an inner GPS system that is so clear and so sure so satisfied excited to get to the destination to experience it faster and enjoying the journey and experiencing contrast still but not getting stuck in such a negative environment people places, things.

Also, learning more along the way and meeting more people without the pain of making so many bad choices that send you spiraling down instead of up. Taking the easier road would be able to feel your way through so much more clearly and appreciating where you came from, and having the understanding that life isn't supposed to be a struggle, but you chose to make it a struggle because you were unconscious most of the way. And I realized I chose to be stuck on the slow boat for twenty-five years, mostly because I was under the influence of a substance that kept me drifting slowly to my destination.

Well, with this knowledge. it is my hope and wish for you the reader, you get off and take the jet now if that sounds familiar to you. In today's world if you seek the truth you will find it there's no reason to not be leveling up right now and bettering yourself we came to this matrix to have fun and master growth. We didn't come here to struggle. We came here to be learning to love and loving to learn is what the awakened soul should be about right now and learning how to be of service to others but first you have to learn how to be of service to yourself by learning yourself that is being of service to yourself only then will you be a whole individual able to attract another partner or soul tribe to match your frequency of love. In order to have successful manifestations, you have to go inward and you have to discover yourself and your desires.

You have to love yourself; you have to uncover limiting beliefs that have been holding you back; you have to reprogram your mind with the new affirmations, tell new stories, and let go of the past so you can create your future.

That's why we should never ever judge where another person is on their journey. Instead, we should try to get more clear about our passions and destination so we can reach for others behind us and help them out. By sharing our experiences, others can relate and then choose to make better choices for themselves. So we can enjoy ourselves while we're here experiencing the human experience together as one collective before the vehicles of these bodies have had enough. I want to finish this existence more satisfied with no regrets. If I haven't completed my soul's missions in this lifetime, at least I can come back as an advanced human because of the levels of consciousness that I had achieved in this last lifetime and really have the time of my life in the next lifetime filled with good karma coming to me.

All of our missions here as a collective consciousness is to become the ultimate beings and reach complete peace in our lives and live higher states of consciousness and love. Life is 10% what happens to you and 90% of how you react to it. Stop thinking you are small you are a part of God's consciousness God sees through your eyes. The power of God is in you. That light shines from you and is eternal light and love, unconditional love you are the creators of your reality. Remember who you are. So you can get off of the slow boat and get onto the jet. Stop being unconscious, and choose to be conscious and present every day. The Journey through the darkness, was the contrast the choices that I made so I could learn from them so I know what I don't want to be. So I can remember my inner light my spiritual love, love for myself and being of service to others. was my personal power that I had been giving away to all the bad choices, and the addiction that kept me in a low vibration state of consciousness.

Now I see the opposite of addiction is spirituality. I now know who I am, and what I am meant to do because of being connected to god/source and fully aware that I am power. I am a spiritual happiness life coach learning from and understanding that the journey through the darkness of my life on the slow boat, to the light of sobriety and connecting with my personal power source is just my beginning. This book is kind of a way of me leaving the past behind me, and stepping into that light fully, the pure, love and light that's in all of us and leaving behind all of my disharmonious choices. I don't like to say bad or good or right or wrong because if you learn from things that you thought were wrong from your own perception, then it never was wrong or bad just disharmonious or low vibration.

I surrendered to my higher self, God's love, so I could stay in alignment in the flow state taking a more harmonious path to have more fun, living for my purpose—instead of going against the flow, struggling to go the opposite direction. Life is supposed to be easy; surrendering to the flow is what I choose to do now; instead of taking that slow boat, with all the obstacles, I choose to enjoy the rest of my life going with ease and comfort to the same destination. I was supposed to be going all along, but now I have no doubts or confusion and no one can take me off my route but me. I am no longer a victim in my life to circumstances. I know now that I am the cocreator of my reality and anything that I attract wanted, or unwanted I manifested with the law of attraction and I own that today and I can see it clearly when it is happening, which helps me bounce back from any negative experiences quicker than I ever did before while I'm enjoying a more satisfying, amazing, happy, joyous, appreciative journey, while taking the jet.

MEDITATION IS THE SECRET KEY TO SUCCESS

Okay, meditation on my YouTube channel Kelly Keith Goddess Coach, you can find a video or two there. I do my morning meditations for fifteen minutes, so simple and easy. Esther Hicks says you wouldn't go to vacuum your carpet and not plug in the vacuum and just push it around all the dirt and just make the lines in the carpet and move it around a little bit; no, you wouldn't do that. You would plug it in first. Okay, here's another example from Esther Hicks. I love this one: You wouldn't go to your car and refuse to bring your keys, so why would you wake up and not meditate and plug yourself in for fifteen minutes a day to your higher self, your higher intelligent part of yourself.

Connect to your guides so you can be in total alignment, tuned in, tapped in, and turned on so you make fewer mistakes throughout the day because you're a built-in GPS system that you connected to first thing in the morning is guiding you to take the right exit off the freeway to avoid a traffic jam to hold on to a rail so you don't fall down the stairs at lunch when you're in a hurry. Every little thing and big thing that could possibly happen that keeps you in alignment because you're making good choices at the spur the moment, makes life so much easier and blissful to live without stress, without being in flight-or-fight mode all day. That is hard on our bodies to live like that. If you're connected, you won't have the stress that you have every day making the wrong choices because you're not connected to anything that you can't see ahead of time.

Meditation changed my life, and it will change yours as well. I can't stress enough how important plugging in to your vortex of source energy will make you feel so high, like really high without a substance. It's real personal power magic. Take your personal power back and plug in to your quiet power place in your mind that has all your answers you could ever want. It's self-love on freaking overload and we all need more self-love right now. I'm going to go over our spiritual twelve universal laws of the universe, the keys to you becoming and having anything you want to be or have. Follow these laws. Learn them first and follow them, which means don't push them aside like they don't matter. Oh, they matter. These I've discovered will help you to become super human. These are the laws of truth or real laws, the ones we should have been taught in school. They're there to help guide us from my understanding. Also, you can find them in a video on YouTube and in the bookstore; anything you want to know today is there.

There's no reason to not be educated. The truth to everything and anything is out there. Just look and I promise you will find it. Nothing is hidden from society anymore because we are in the Aquarius energy, a new earth and that planet is influencing us and it's about expansion and bettering ourselves and evolution. We have movement off the merry-go-round, off of Neptune's energy. It's moving away from us completely now. It was hell, in my opinion. I need constant change in my life in order to grow and so do you. So in the mornings for fifteen minutes, put a timer on your phone, sit down somewhere quiet where you won't be disturbed, get a journal so you can journal afterwards, because any thoughts that come to you afterwards are going to be magical thoughts.

After quieting your mind, even if you can only quiet your mind a little bit, if you get some very powerful inspiration during that time of quiet in your mind this is when Tesla, Edison, Einstein—the great people in history—this is when they got their inventions and secret knowledge from their higher selves through meditation. Do not minimize meditation or push it off as if it's just a word people say a lot of things about it. But I can't stress enough how powerful it is and how it was the key to my successes and to my growth as a human, having a human experience. This was the key to knowing when to act having inspired ideas. That works every time. I promise you, you will not regret it. I'm high on life every day, excited to wake up. I'm never bored because I am in total alignment with source energy, because I wake up and meditate for fifteen minutes every day and you can too.

12 SPIRITUAL LAWS
TO LEARN

#1) The law of oneness = We are all one and the same, a creator, all connected. We are all source energy. We are a different part of consciousness, so consciousness can be experienced in all different ways. Different perceptions but all the same.

#2) The law of vibration = Everything is energy so all you have to do is match the energy if you want something—be it money, love, material things—all you have to do is match the feeling of energy of what you want and it's yours you can use affirmation frequencies; get on the vibration of the material thing or place that you want and it becomes a magnet. It's the law.

#3) The law of ACTION = Inspirational action, inner guidance, system check your feelings. If it feels good, do it. If it feels burdensome, then don't. When you trust the feelings, then act. Get connected to it. It will never lead you wrong. Your gut instinct? Trust it. Grow your intuition by only acting when it feels good.

#4) The law of correspondence = As above, so below. In here reality creates your outer world. What do you want? Focus on what you want not what has become and be aware of your thoughts.

#5) The law of cause and effect = No blaming or playing victim. Take responsibility. Focus on your desires powerless personal power cause-and-effect, think opposites of everything, become aware of karma. To be safe just give love unconditionally.

#6) The law of compensation = This is how you can learn to have faith in the unseen (blessings, rewards). Be aware when you're feeling satisfying feelings and when they come back to you and then being thankful for what you have brought to you from cause-and-effect and or, as us humans call it— good and bad. Become aware so you can change it fast and receive your rewards.

#7) The law of ATTRACTION = All matter, aka material, comes back to you—the energy you put out, thoughts, feelings, action, positive people or negative people? Understand so you can make a new perception feel, talk, act, and tell your story how you want it to be, not how it actually is. You will attract the story you are in the present moment telling over and over and over again. It's the law in the unseen world.

#8) The law of perpetual transmutation of energy = You can start over, change anytime (hard reset), embrace change. Fear just holds you back. Be aware, be awakened to the truth. Life is not a merry-go-round. If you don't like what you see, change it. You can restart your day at any time. You do not have to have twenty-four hours of a bad day, just an example a small one.

#9) The law of relativity = Understanding that we all have differentperspectives and subjective experiences, can help you have empathyfor others. Time and space are a concept.

#10) The law of polarity = Focus on present moment feelings in the present moment, what feels satisfying and great and what doesn't feel so great—knowing, letting go, having boundaries and, yes, change it in the now to an action of what you do want. Don't wait. The present is all you have. The only thing that's real is today, this moment and emotions always in motion in this moment.

#11) The law of rhythm = Understand the seasons: meditation, connection to source energy, highs and lows—knowing them and when it's a time for transformation understanding when change is needed.

#12) The law of gender = Ying yang masculine and feminine. Feminine = Creative Masculine = action; you need to have your intuitive and creative side and your action and discipline side of your personality. We all have masculine and feminine in our personalities. You have to own both. It's the law in the unseen world.

Understanding these laws will help you in your personal development and your self-discovery and gaining your personal power and in creating your reality the way you desire it to be. I wish you all the joy and happiness on your adventures in learning these laws and creating your world. If you desire to have a life coach, you can contact me at unitylovelifecoaching.com or on any of my social media platforms or you could just go to my You-Tube channel (Kelly Keith Goddess Coach). Please help me out and support me by subscribing to my channel so you can get my new content. I'm trying to post a video every day now.

If you enjoyed this book, please tell a friend. I hope my learning lessons—that have made me who I am today—can help you in some way. If it just helps one person to either stay safe in the game or to make more money or just relate to me, then this is a little treasure I'm proud I shared.

I'm about helping others find their personal path and purpose because I've found mine and I'm learning unconditional love to all humanity and all living things. I do not judge another because of my experiences and I hope that I will not be judged as well. What I want is for people to be able to relate to me on a deeper level. A lot of life coaches tell their story so others could learn who they are and what they're about so you can see if you can relate to the life coach that you're considering hiring before you hire them. Writing this book is a way for me to end the struggles in life, kind of an ending to the old me when I was young and immature and reckless.

I had to go through these lessons because of my choices and this is just my beginning. I have no desire at all to use anything that takes me out of my mind, body, soul connection. After twenty years of using, the addiction lost its power over me. I want to help anybody who is ready to be sober and is struggling. Also people who want to awaken to their greatness because I have found mine. I am happy every day; even my bad days are really not that bad. They don't last as long and I wish that for others as well. I don't have any regrets in my life. I am happy to share my story with you. Thank you for being part of my journey. And if nobody's told you today, I love you and continue learning to love and loving to learn.

KELLY KEITH

12 STEPS, NONTRADITIONAL RECOVERY

So I've created 12 non-traditional recovery steps that worked for me. Based off of new age, principles and exercises that you can do on a dayto-day basis. Some steps that I use are the same as the traditional 12 steps but from my perspective with more relatable ways of acting on the step.

#1 STEP ADMITTING

Admitting you have a problem

An that you are an addict out loud. Or admitting that you have relapsed to someone you love is the very first step. I was really good at hiding my addiction and I'm not delusional. When I finally admitted to my kids and their friends, that I had been using all these years they had no idea, I proceeded to tell them details which surprised them even more. Me confessing in detail was me really being done. I wasn't trying to just take a break. Me saying all my secrets was showing I was done because now I would be called out for any of that behavior again. So in order to save yourself and be your own hero you need to confess all you have done with using drugs to loved ones for their support. All the people that you kept in the dark for one reason or another need to know the truth. The truth needs to come to light. Your personal power is taken back by releasing and freeing yourself from the lies. So just know if you're not ready to let yourself free by admitting it out loud to loved ones that you have a problem, then you're not fully ready for a change yet. I am just trying to be real honest here and that's what you are gonna have to do. By getting honest with yourself first then your loved ones frees your soul. living in denial is no way to live. Telling the truth and living a honest life changes the game of life you have been living for the better.

#2 STEP FAITH IN SOMETHING (Unseen)
In traditional 12 steps they say to believe in a higher power I like that but it's not a modern way of saying it. I had a girlfriend who believes in trees I believe in everything as universal consciousness. we are a small part of source energy experiencing itself through our eyes and perception . We are all one with source energy. Unconditional love energy and so intern I believe in all things godly or good. We are all different perspectives of God's con-sciousness. A belief is only some thing you keep

thinking which gives it power to be real so to have faith in some thing you cannot see connects you with your personal power. Your higher self is your higher intelligence the source part of all of us. When we look outside of ourselves that's when we attract people places things a.k.a. (Drugs) to fill the empty void we feel from not having faith in our (higher self) I'm calling it higher self because I can relate to that better but you can call it whatever you wish there is never only one way. There's always different perspectives and ways of doing things I believe we are all equal just on different levels of maturity and growth and so we should never judge others for where they are because they are just on a different level than you. Having faith That infinite intelligence will have your back is very powerful to believe in so that is why it is a must to stay sober. To have faith is to be spiritually connected to something bigger. It has worked for me and it has helped me grow and I can now see the light out of the darkness. I don't fear anything I feel so empowered with love and focus I don't feel any need to look back at the life I used to live numbed out and lost and confused because I have a belief in source, universal consciousness, unconditional love, the unseen the life force that created all of us.

#3 STEP Prayer ,intentions, meditation
Learning how to pray. Intending to be protected and guided and given the strength to get through the day is another way of asking for God's will to shine on you.(Thanking) source or God, whatever you want to call higher intelligence is a way of Praying. Thanking source for keeping you aware and fully conscious throughout your day. Thanking source for showing you signs and magic throughout the day. Asking for guidance and inspired action . Then going into meditation. Start with five minutes after a month move to 10 minutes after another month. Move to 15 minutes. Then you clear your mind get comfortable second put a timer on your phone then you start it. Clear your mind focus on a steady sound in your environment so an air conditioning is good or your breath breathing in and out I go back-andforth between the air conditioner and my breath. Have a notebook and pen ready for any thoughts that follow your meditation or during so you can remember it for later, and then go back to paying attention to your breath or the air conditioner. The reason to write these things down, so that way you can quiet your mind again because you're ego trying ,to control your thoughts. Any messages that come following meditation after you

quiet your mind are powerful messages from your higher self coming through to guide you. It doesn't happen right away but after doing this first thing in the morning every day for 30 days or more you will get more and more clear on what you want in life. There are several different ways to do meditation you can try them all to see which One is best for you. People say the hardest one is quieting your mind and they say that it's the most beneficial. I agree The one I just gave you details on how to do is the best one from my perception. This is the one that I do every day no matter what . Another meditation is listening to someone guide you into it this I feel is really good to start with they're called guided meditations. There are so many free ones on YouTube. Remember anytime you are learning something new enjoy the journey. Another one is a meditation walk just go on a 10 or 15 minute walk barefoot and really be present during your walk enjoy it use all your senses, hearing smelling, touching, seeing all the beauty in the world at that very moment. Let time just disappear. Another form of meditation is singing out loud doesn't matter the song doesn't matter if you are good at it. Just sing from your belly and feel every word. It has to be a song you know the words to. Another form of meditation is yoga or dance. So in my experience from quitting my mind meditation, it was so amazing I'll never forget it. I felt so high vibe I felt so happy. I felt so calm and balanced and just happy like nobody could bring me down. I was so connected to everything I didn't feel any restlessness or confusion. I felt total love and clarity I was so peaceful. Now don't do anything in excess and this includes meditation doing more than 40 minutes in a day you will get blissed out and feel not centered you will feel like you are not in your body and unable to think people will start asking if you are high again if you do that. 15 minutes a day is best at least from my perception it's best for me. There's no one way but I am just giving you some info I was given and what worked for me. OK so Abraham/Esther hicks says if you wouldn't go vacuum your floor and refuse to plug in your vacuum and just make the marks on the floor moving dirt around, why not refuse to start your day without plugging yourself into higher intelligence first thing in the morning also she says you would not go to leave in your car and refuse to take your keys so why not get up a little earlier to plug yourself into source energy. It made clear sense to me when I heard it put like that. The benefits are great because you have infinite intelligence guiding you and you're aware of it all day. So you will be guided to take an exit off the freeway just in time to miss the accident ahead of you. Or you will remember your glasses before you leave your house when you're running late somewhere. You will be on time more. You will make better choices at a moments notice. So why not it prevents unwanted obstacles in your life that you have grown used to but shouldn't be accepting in life. Life is supposed to be easier and more enjoying then the stressful path you are already on. We didn't come here wanting to experience life struggles we came here to have fun and learn from our contrast and creating from what we don't want by learning what we do desire from experiencing what we don't want we learn what we do want. But it's supposed to be fun the whole time learning how to enjoy the journey no matter what the circumstances. Bashar says circumstances don't matter only my state of being matters. What state of being do I prefer?Is a statement that we should repeat to ourselves, so we don't take life so seriously and then asking ourselves what state of being do I prefer will help to always have control over how you are feeling. I prefer being connected to my inner child , trying to have more fun, not being naïve, but being fully aware that I am choosing a more peaceful, fun state of being. Anyway you understand . Prayers are a way to connect with source energy and build a relationship intentions is another form of prayer meditation is a way to total alignment with source energy . Infinite intelligence

#4 STEP JOURNALING

Journaling helps you get out of your mind and into a flow state it's easier to process your thoughts and feelings, and to record your progress and also helps with manifestation. Journaling helps. You get your personal power back by connecting you to mind, body and soul. There's power be hind the action of writing your thoughts onto paper. It will help you process trauma, feelings of sadness and grief, but it can also help you get clear on what you want in your present moment, and for your future based off of past experiences that you write down.

Now there are so many ways to journal and I do them all but I like to write. If you don't enjoy writing you can talk text inyour notes on your phone. The power you get from putting your Thoughts down with pen and paper is magical. In the morning I start with segment intending after I do my 15 minutes of meditation I create my morning with I am statements about a paragraph long. About how I want my morning and afternoon to feel I try to start with feeling words here's an example I am really going to enjoy making breakfast for my son and when I wake him up he is so sweet to me and respectful and we both enjoyed our drive together on our way to his school and I hit more green lights and he got there on time. So instead of having a crazy emotional morning I take control and created my morning instead of life happening to me and me being a victim I am the creator of my reality OK so you can do that throughout your day or with important trips and see how it all plays out exactly, or even better than you had planned . Play with this have fun.

Another way of journaling is gratitude journal so at night before bed write out 10 things you are grateful for or thankful for this makes your vibration higher before you go to bed it puts you in total alignment with source energy and then you will wake up in total alignment it gives you a Headstart for your next day. If you're somebody that wakes up moody and grumpy and not wanting to get out of bed that will change if you start with the list of thankful things before you go to sleep it's guaranteed try it.

A dream journal is great to keep by your bed because you can go back and get messages about how you felt yesterday a dream analysis college course I took 10 years ago I learned this exercise about dreams I'm going to tell it to you now by dissecting your feelings from each event in the story you write down after you first wake up and use feeling words so for an example here's a dream that I had and I wrote down right when I woke up you just write down whatever comes to mind even if it doesn't make sense just write it down so here's my dream I had example I was driving down My dads Street with my cousin who was in prison and then there was a baby and I saw the baby at the house but we left then we realize the baby got left alone and we hurried back and I woke up.

(Feeling words)break up each individual event in the dream

I was driving down my dad's old Street= werid , confused

Cuzin= I was happy

A baby= I felt concern

Then we left and I realize we left the baby alone= I got scared,worried

OK so then you ask yourself where yesterday did I feel weird confused happy concerned, scared and worried Bam I remembered a conversation I had with my babies dad at dinner the night before that I didn't share with anybody. My subconscious wanted me to remember how I felt the day before so I could process the situation so see only 1% of the time will it be a dream of a future event. Putting Pen and paper by your bed and asking your subconscious mind right before you go to sleep to help you remember your dreams and the action of putting the paper and pen by your bed is the keys to remembering your dreams again and getting messages of how you were feeling yesterday.

Journaling during a new moon make a list of 10 things you want to stop doing then make a list of 10 things you want to start doing. Rip up the things that you wanna stop doing and throw them away or burn them if you can safely the things you want to stop doing Forget about them. The 10 things you want to start doing read them every morning till you start seeing changes. Keep them under your pillow or by your bed so you remember."

Keep them under your pillow or by your bed so you remember to readthem in the morning until you start to see the changeshappening.

you can also just journal about your day at the end

of every day just a paragraph sums it up so you can remember yesterday and last week so you can build your memory back after all the damage to our brains from the drug abuse or alcohol abuse whatever your abuse was .

It will take one year for your memory and brain cells to fully restore themselves.

#5 STEP Ho'oponopono

The ho'oponopono is a Hawaiian prayer that you can look up and get allthe history behind it. I always suggest looking things up and not takingsomeone's word for it investigate. Or use your intuition what feels right to you. Ho'onponopono means (To make right) in the Hawaiian language which translates into you taking 100% responsibility for what you have attracted, owning that somewhere in your subconscious mind there are beliefs that need to be cleared and wounds that need to behealed. It's you realigning with the truth of who you are, releasing the illusion of separation from the other and coming back into the present moment with a blank slate. It's you getting back to zero Wise, which is a state of being pure love, thought ego free and in the present. From here inspiration can flow. If loved and cared for the subconscious becomes anally. Period. (Dr. Hew Len)

The basic ideas except everything that is in your life instead of pushingthings off on others or blaming circumstances you take responsibility for them you first remind yourself that you are worthy of love and that loveallows you to ask for forgiveness to release events in your life it is only through excepting total responsibility that you can attract true miracles to you.

Do it by saying the following four phrases like a mantra in your mind or out loud repeating it over and over I love you I'm sorry please forgive me thank you I love you I'm sorry please forgive me thank you you are directing the phrases to the emotional trigger i.e. The undesired feelings, the subconscious mind, and the divine. Here's a bit more on what is behind each of the four phrases.

I love you- I see that we are love, And I vow again to remember that Love is the only thing that is real. I choose love. Love will transform this.

I'm sorry − I take 100% responsibility and ownership from my perspective and my part, for going unconscious, for believing in the illusion of separation, for choosing fear instead of love.

Please forgive me − I correct my vision and I see what's real eternal. I understand and I'm recommitted to releasing the illusion and toremembering the truth – we are one in the presence of love.

Thank you – I am grateful for this lesson and for this realignment with love.

Now there is no reason to big or to small

It can be used when a person cut you off on the freeway. It can be used when you're upset about something your boss said. Think of how many small moments we deal with every day and how they affect us. If you have the power to create a positive experience, then why wouldn't you do it? Simply by not reacting, taking responsibility, and knowing that you can affect your own outlet, as well as that of others, you begin to understand the true-power behind this ancient knowledge.

No matter where you are, adverse things happen during the course of a day. When confronted with such events, this technique will allow you to release the events and to open yourself up to the good in every situation. We live in a world that is driven by beliefs, beliefs about who we are, what we do, and what we can accomplish. The law of attraction works by bringing us everything we think about, even those things that are hidden within our subconscious mind. This is a tool that helps clear away those subconscious ideas that we aren't even aware of, so we can attract all the good things that we want to our lives.

Dr. Hew Len, taught this clearing method it comes from his lineage. The only purpose in your life and mine is the restoration of our identity – our mind – back to its original state of void or zero (Buddha), Of purity of heart (Shakespeare)through nonstop cleaning.

It is the void, as zero, where divine love resides, providing inspiration for a perfect relationship, perfect health and perfect wealth.

The responsibility and the function of the conscious mind intellect are:

#1. To initiate the cleaning,

#2. To care for the subconscious,

#3. Teach it the cleansing process and

#4. To ask divinity for directions

The conscious mind is coolest as to what memories are replaying (11,000,000 per second) in the subconscious. Only divine love can transmit toxic memories to pure energies. Divine love is the only source of inspiration and enlightenment! The conscious mind does not perform these functions! The subconscious, as the super computer, is the key to the self identity through a ho'oPonopono cleansing process. If loved and cared for, the subconscious becomes an ally, cleansing nonstop even as we sleep.

#6 STEP EFT
(EMOTIONAL FREEDOM TAPPING)

Eft this is letting go of past trauma by tapping on pressure points on your face and neck. You will need to make a list of things after you understand what traumas and blockages you might have from reading further.

You'll probably agree that in this day when life runs on adrenaline, youneed to have solid stress management mechanisms in place. Self-help-methods have become important life skills. That is where emotional freedom technique EFT tapping comes in. Think of EFT has a reset button at your fingertips. EFT is an amazing self-help technique millions are using worldwide. Tapping can be used for relief from sadness, fear, worry, anxiety, anger, phobias, bad habits and performance issues naturally. You can use EFT for relief from negative emotions and a host of physical problems. It works by dissolving energy blocks when you tap on certain points on your face and body. It can help you bring more love, happiness, confidence and money into your life. This incredible method is about dramatic, lasting changes, fast. What is EFT? EFT stands for emotional freedom technique or tapping. EFT is a powerful self-help method based on research showing that emotional trauma contributes greatly to disease. Stanford engineer Gary Craig developed EFT as a self-help tool for people struggling with painful emotions that traditional medical and psychological treatments had been unable to help. It is said that intense negative emotions, if not processed and dealtwith, can get stuck in our energy body. This negative emotions then color our view of the world, intern attracting more of the same. Long-term stress and bottled up emotions lead to diseases. This is not to say that we shouldn't feel any negative emotions or being in denial about hurtful emotions. We just need to find a healthy way to experience and expunge negative emotion so they don't get stored in our mind body system. You have to use a tool to expunge negative emotions. Who invented EFT? In the 80s, Doctor. Roger Callahan invented thought field therapy or TFT, which is known as the Precuror to eft. Gary Craig, the inventor of EFT, trained under Doctor. Callahan. He later branched outwith his own version of tapping therapy which we know as EFT.

EFT by far is the easiest yet most comprehensive tool for regular people like you and me. It is handy, there are no complex algorithms involved, it is easily accessible, and easily learned.

Think of EFT as an open source of self development tool. As long as you don't start calling yourself the creator of EFT, you can do pretty much anything you like with it. The other problem with many of the other tapping modalities is that the onlyway to learn them is to get professional certification even if you just want them for your personal use. That is often the only way to get detailed information about them or, you have to go to practitioner who is certified in that technique. That is sort of a guarded approach prevents miss use and misinterpretation of a technique, but it also creates a walled garden around it. For just trying out some thing, you should not have to get professional certification. It's like needing to become a pro chef if you want to start cooking in your own kitchen! Thankfully, EFT can be learned and used free of cost from the comfortof your own home. How does EFT work EFT/tapping works by dissolvingenergy blockages when you tap on certain points on your face and body. That helps you to clear out all the stress, worry, anxiety and fear, so you automatically make space for more love, happiness, success and moremoney in your life. A deeper explanation relies on a network of energy channels running through the body – the Meridian system. Like blood vessels carry blood, meridians carry energy. Negative emotions create energy blockages in the meridian system. EFT unclogs and balances the meridian system as you tap on certain points while focusing on an issue. A modern explanation about why an EFT tapping works is based on a part of the brain called the amygdala. EFT tapping, by the virtue of gentle tapping movements, calms our fight – or flight response. That intern allows a rational part of the brain to Conger solutions that we're not available to it when it was subjected to stress and negative emotions. Another theory is that tapping movement on the surface of the skin generate light electrical impulses which then get transmitted to the brain. That's the mind – body connection. Yes he relies on our ability to tune in to our negative emotions of sadness, anger frustration etc. For example tapping while using a reminder phrase such as so disappointed with the result doesn't sound very cheerful does it? If you are from the Law Of Attraction line of thinking, or simply a positive thinker, you might wonder why we are focusing so much on ranting out negative thoughts. The thing is, EFT is a cleansing technique. You bring up negative emotions to the surface and clear them out from the root. For the record it is safe to focus on the negative while tapping. While tapping you bring up negative emotions to the surface and then clear them out. After that you plant some positive empowering choices in their place. Itis like going to a doctor or healer. If you are only going to tell them what is already healthy, they can't help you. You need to tell them what's wrong. When we are not tapping, it serves us to hold the highest and best thoughts possible. But during tapping, focus as much as you can on-what makes you feel bad and stuck until you feel ready to move on to some positive tapping. Signs that show EFT is working we all need to know when something is working, and the more the physical evidence of it, the better. Luckily there are some physical signs that indicate that your tapping efforts are bearing fruit and energy is shifting. Mind you, not all the signs are necessary for effectiveness of tapping and not all signs will show up in one single tapping session. It may be that you will experience some of the signs quite often and others in frequently, or never also, you may very well experience other physical sensations that are specific to your energetics constitution. Learning to identify the sensations will help you become more confident about your application of tapping one of the signs that I noticed in my own tapping is that once I have tapped enough, I get the urge to get up and walk around my room a little bit maybe have a sip of water. And then I fear back to where I was sitting and get tapping again it seems to me that this re-adjust my energy in someway and I feel more bal-ance after a little movement. Here are 12 of the common sign showing that tapping is repairing energy disruptions in your body.

Gasping a exhale of surprise, sighing an in-hale of relief or boredom, yawning energy is shift-ing, tears or watery eyes, coughing, lump in the throat clearing, not in the chest clearing, a buzzing feeling through the body, shoulders dropping, sleep-iness, tiredness, sudden pain relief. No if an issue was getting cleared there are eight major indicators of whether an issue has been completely cleared or not. Often it can be just a knowing, accompanied by feeling of relief it may feel like a load has been-lifted off your shoulders. Clearly this is a very sub-jective indicator before you start tapping give the issue a number on a scale of 0 to 10 based on how bad you were feeling 10 being unbearable zero being totally fine. This one involves recalling the details of an event or abothersome issue as if you were describing it to a friend. If an issue was resolved, you may notice that you are you're not even able to concentrate on describing the event without getting distracted. Your attention keeps slipping from the thoughts of that event to things iny our environment. It is as if you have disconnected yourself from that event and discharging all the pain and negativity through tapping. You feel bored talking about that issue but if you are still passionate about what you were talking about and feel feelings of anger or sadness behind it then you need to tap again it didn't work. As you start to explore more of tapping, you will come across this and famous phrase root cause. It is said that eliminating the root cause of a problem using tapping removes all traces of the problem from your life, mind and body. It sounds like something we need to take seriously. Accessing the root cause of a problem and tapping on the roots events related to That can bring profound results with EFT tapping. A Root cause when it comes to EFT tapping, has a negative believe required at some point in time that is still running your life. It can go back to the time when you acquired that belief, and change the belief, you could change the course of your life. Here are two ways to look at a root cause #1 a root cause can be a set of thoughts. Say, you have been trying to lose some weight, with unsatisfactory results. Or that you lose some weight, but gain it back within no time. As you sit down to lock in on the root cause of the weight issue, you may notice that you were actually afraid to lose weight. Because if you did men would want to flirt with you all the time. Or that peoples expectations of you would rise in some way. The root cause in this case is the belief that your life will become difficult if you lose weight if you start to think that the problem was not a big deal in the first place you've definitely cleared it that is because the changes with tapping happen at such a deep level that our thoughts about that issue change, often completely and ending with a positive bent. Laughter also indicates emotional clearing. You may notice yourself breaking into spontaneous bouts of laughter as you weretapping. It indicates that the clouds of negative emotions are lifting. You may notice a change in your own behavior from then onwards. This change will be most prominent during the first few times after the tapping. After some time, the new behavior will come naturally and you will hardly notice it. Things may start to move differently as well. When you try to think of the issue your thoughts may be automatically followed by the positive reframes that rose up during tapping. If you were afraid you were going to turn out like your mom you may get reminded of the reframe that you are nothing like your mom and that you turned out quite OK. Imagery that you see in your mind when you think of an issue may change to a more positive or compassionate one. If before tapping you thought of you as a child and an accident and all you could see in your mind's eye was the image of you falling off a bicycle, it may now change the memory of how your father gently picked you up and you were fine. This memory of your father would be the image of what really happened, not an illusion. It is just that the mind has learned to focus on a positive aspect of the incident. So when youl ook back at that child incident, you feel safe and cared for instead of shocked and hurt. Tapping on the secondary benefit will release the fear.

#2. A root cause can be a past event. It is possible that at some point in the past when you were at your ideal weight, something bad happened. Say your boyfriend parted ways with you. That may not have been related to your weight at all. But that is the way you're mind sees it. So when you neutralize your emotions around that break up event, your belief ideal weight=rejection Will wither in the process. It is likely that you will reach your ideal weight then it is possible to tap on a problem without probing into a root cause. Though that can be like trying to collapse a tree by breaking off one leaf at a time. A root cause is literally the roots of a tree on which all problems originated from the root cause-grow as leaves. For example a colleague at work past the remark about your incompetence and you really took it to heart. You could tap on this issue and release all emotional charge around it and that would be all. When it would be helpful to dig deeper and see if there could be something else contributing to this emotional injury. As you sit down to tap on a problem notice your thoughts about it. Does this issue make you feel good or bad? If bad, then which part of the problem is most hurtful? This question often uncovers how you feel about a problem. Another way to uncover emotions is to simply ask yourself, how does this problem make me feel? The ideas not so much to name a feeling as it is to feel the feeling, whatever it is add, as you tap. It is good if you can put a finger on exactly what emotion you are feeling. But it is not necessary. You felt rejected when you were passed over for a promotion. You also felt disappointed. Naming a feeling helps you focus on that feeling while you tap. That way you know exactly when that feeling has been neutralized and you are ready to tackle other aspect of that issue. Naming an emotion if you cannot come up with the name of an emotion try saying out exactly as you see the problem. The examples below show various ways in which we can describe our problems without pinpointing the underlying emotions. I feel trapped in thesituation emotion powerlessness, it feels like a heavy load on my chestemotion overwhelmed, so many things could go wrong emotion worry, your nagging chokes me emotion anger frustration, there is no way I can do this emotion despair, I feel like I'm shooting in the dark emotion uncertainty, tapping script (10 rounds) the goal of this sample tapping script is to help you release feelings of guilt over something that you should've done but didn't. we all make mistakes from time to time we all miss out on doing things we should've done caring the guilt and regret over what we should've done only weighs us down. It is also detrimental to developing a healthy self-esteem. The way to use the script is to bring to mind a situation where you should've done some thing for example, you should have :

Taken a certain action when it was time say filing taxes timely, spoken up when it was needed say stepping up and excepting your mistake, done something, but at that time you didn't know you needed to do it.

The third point above is important because we often blame ourselves of inaction When we didn't even know we needed to do some thing! Yes, ignorance is no excuse, but how long should we punish ourselves for our ignorance? The kind of incidence you can tap on using the script don't have to be major life changing ones, although they can be. Even seemingly small incidence can leave behind a heavy load of regret. So pick any in action that you're still blaming yourself for, and tap along.

EFT tapping round 1

Eyebrow – I should've done it.

Side of the eye – I should have.

Under the eye – but I didn't.

Under the nose – I should've done it.

Chin – I let things slide.

Collarbone – I had the chance.

Under the arm – this guilt.

Top of the head- this shame.

EFT tapping round 2

Eyebrow – this regret.

Side of the eye – this anger.

Under the eye– this brutality.

Under the nose – it is weighing me down.

Chin – I feel horrible.

Collarbone – I should've known better. Under the arm – I feel stupid.

Top of the head look at this mess now.

EFT tapping round 3

eyebrow – I'm surprised I didn't do it.

Side of the eye – I should've done it.

Under the eye – I had the chance.

Under the nose – I blew it.

Chin – that in action.

Collarbone – that laziness.

Under the arm – that ignorance.

Top top of the head – that Forgetfulness.

EFT tapping round 4

Eyebrow – that withholding.

Side of the eye – it cost me much.

Under the eye – I knew this was coming.

Under the nose – I should've done it.

Chin – that carelessness.

KELLY KEITH

Collarbone – this disappointment.

Under the arm – this pain.

Top of the head – the shame.

EFT tapping round 5

Eyebrow – the shame.

Side of the eye the scale.

Under the eye – this anger.

Under the nose – this brutality.

Chin – this regret.

Collarbone – I let myself down.

Under the arm – I should've done it.

Top of the head – I did not take it seriously.

EFT tapping around 6

Eyebrow – I should've done it.

Side of the eye – I should've stepped up.

Under the eye – I should have Stepped up.

Under the nose – I should have used more sense.

– I didn't know any better.

Chin – my in action made everything complicated.

Collarbone – I'm ashamed.

Under the arm – I pride myself on doing the right things.

Top of the head – but here I failed myself.

EFT tapping round 7

Eyebrow – how will I ever get over it?

Side of the eye – I will never get over it.

Under the eye – I should've taken a chance.

Under the nose – but I'm only human.

Chin – humans make mistakes.

Collarbone – I don't know of a single person.

Under the arm – who hasn't made a mistake in their life.

Top of the head – people make mistakes.

EFT tapping round 8

Eyebrow – people repeat mistakes.

Side of the eye – what if I could keep the learning.

Under the eye – and let the same go?

Under the nose – that doesn't mean.

Chin – I will never make mistakes again. Collarbone – I will make mistakes.

Under the arm – and it is OK .

Top of the head – no really, it is.

EFT tapping round 9

Eyebrow – what is not OK.

Side of the eye – is constantly beating myself up.

Under the eye – maybe I can forgive myself.

Under the nose – I forgive myself.

Chin – everything is forgiven.

KELLY KEITH

Collarbone – I'm feeling better.

Under the arm – I'm feeling lighter.

Top of the head – I forgive others who may be involved.

EFT tapping around 10

Eyebrow – I choose to look ahead.

Side of the eye – and do what I can to make things better.

Under the eye – I choose to be more discerning in the future.

Under the nose-but I also know that good judgment.

Chin –it is not a club to hold over my head.

Collarbone – I choose to loosen up a bit. Under the arm – I choose to be free.

Top of the head – I choose to be calm an confident.

Tap along to this script a few more times until all emotional charge around your inaction has diffuse and you feel way better tips on tapping you use tapping action to stimulate the acupuncture points located in an area that helps to dislodge energy blockages, which intern clears negative emotions. How many taps per point? Tap approximately seven times on each point. It is perfectly OK if you tap more than that. You do not need to say the reminder phrase seven times, you only need to tap each EFT point approximately seven times while saying the reminder phrase. Tapping for at least 5 to 6 rounds on any problem is a good idea even if you start to feel better within the first round or two. Your pattern of thoughts will change as you continue tapping on a problem. If a problem resurfaces, it is most likely because some important aspect of it were left untapped. How much force? As you tap you should feel a little bit of bounce back from your skin with tapping more force does not necessarily mean more benefit ideas to feel the stimulation of the tapping points. This stimulation can be felt through a buzzing sensation or an increase blood flow in that area. As you stimulate these points, your feelings will start to change to you . You will start to feel calmer about whatever it is you're tapping about . Tapping amnesia because negativity clears up at a deeper level when you use EFT, you may feel so much lighter afterwards that you may not believe how much an issue used to bother you and what big shifts tapping has created. Since your thoughts about that problem have changed that problem no longer looks like the sword hanging over your head that it once used to, it is easy to downplay the role of tapping. This may keep you from using tapping the next time something bothers you since you won't think tapping as being very powerful. Often, the changes that happen as the result of tapping can seem so natural that you think nothing of them it has happen with me many times.

benefits after I did this I cried and cried and cried I released years of tears that my hard ass had numbed out and buried I felt so light after and happy and free I didn't repeat things stories from my past and communication I had no passion charging the communication of any event anymore I healed myself of all deep rooted pain and sadness that was coming out as anger I was able to start really loving myself and life and others after because I took the time to become present with the pain for 40 minutes with a list of 20 things events and traumas that took place in my life. That I needed to let go of and did In 40 mins. Instead two years in therapy or 10 years some people go to therapy for way to long. I'm not saying therapy is bad but give yourself a 90 day limit to how long you're going to continue to vent about a problem in therapy. The more you talk about a problem the more a problem Persist.learn to let go. Tapping can help that.

#7 STEP Limiting beliefs

How do you create reality beliefs are how we create reality . At the same time a belief is just some thing soneone keeps thinking, so why limit yourself with negative beliefs. you've probably noticed that some people seem to have the same reoccurring problems. Did you ever wonder why it's often the same problem patterns for each person. The person with money problems repeatedly experiences money problems, and the person with relationship Problems frequently runs into relationship problems? It says though each person specializes in there disorder. Internal beliefs are creating the circumstances. Until the dysfunctional beliefs that create the unfortunate events are reprogrammed, the behavior patterns will continue to emerge. Notice, that perception and belief are the beginning of the experience we create. Your beliefs generate your emotions which create your feelings and thoughts which catalyze your behavior whether words or actions, which then finally create your reality we are often unaware of our limiting beliefs because they were passed down to us by the attitudes and beliefs of others. As long as they remain unconscious we are not aware of them they can hold us back from achieving our fullest Potential and experiencing joy.

For example if we have heard all of our life that money is the root of evil then we may unconsciously create situations that limit our financial success out of fear of that evil. Below is a list of some common Phrases that we are often told growing up or here in our community they are so normal that we rarely question their validity Or consider how they affect our belief systems or make us unhappy. Of course there is some truth and a good intention behind most of them, but consider which ones you have been conditioned to believe and how they have impacted your beliefs and your life. here are some examples. and a few solutions to the first few after that think of your own solutions of how you could correct your thinking about that negative limiting belief that's been holding you back.

Money is the root of all evil,

what this is saying

good intention money does not bring happiness and can corrupt conditioned fear negative association with having money it turns you into a bad person potential limits unconsciously avoiding or sabotaging financial success to avoid the negative qualities you believe you'll develop if you have money. Solution,

So if you have this belief, whenever it comes

up, become aware of it, and instead say out loud, with money I can help a lot of people I can accomplish more with money, money brings comfort money brings luxury I can do more in my life with money.

finish your plate. There are starving people in the world.what this is saying,

Good intention don't be wasteful with food and have compassion for others, condition fear food sacriristity or guilt for having more opportunity than others. Potential limits over eating and health problems or holding yourself back to avoid feeling guilty over having more opportunity than others. Solution.

All you have to do is become aware of this if this comes up during the day again, you say instead out loud I love food and food loves me. There's enough to eat. I am always satisfied with the amount that I eat there's always more I always eat what I need to eat, nothing more nothing less the universe is abundant.

Money doesn't grow on trees,

What this is saying

Good intention be intelligent with how you spend your money, condition fear money sacristy feeling that there is not enough and it is hard to get, potential limits not believing you can have what you want if it involves having money and therefore not going for it.

Solution Become aware when this message comes up again and instead of saying this message to yourself say money actually does grow on trees because money is made from paper and paper comes from trees money can flow from multiple resources. I love money and money loves me it ebbs and flows from me effortlessly. I always have enough I am a money magnet.

don't burn your bridges,

What this is saying

Good intention keep good relationships with people who may one day be a resource conditioned fear apprehension to do what you know is right for you if you feel it will make someone disapprove of or reject you, potential limits not making a change or taking an opportunity when it comes out of fear or disappointing, offending or otherwise burning a bridge. solution,

Becoming aware that you are about to say this (don't burn your bridges)instead say I always stand up for myself and if I feel some thing is not right or someone is not right for me, I have to set boundaries for myself and my energy needs to be protected. I have the ability to recognize what is good for me and what is not.

no pain no gain,

Good intention reward is worth a struggle, condition fear the belief that in order to be successful one must suffer, potential limits choosing not to make changes or go for what you want because you feel it will be difficult or painful, holding yourself back from success. solution,

Instead of saying no pain no gain tell yourself

If I follow my highest excitement,and if I always am acting on my highest excitement I can achieve anything

life is hard,

Good intention pain and struggle are a normal part of being human, conditioned fear there is no hope of you feelingsatisfied or happy in life, potential limits feeling discouraged and hopeless excepting difficulties or unnecessary suffering because you believe it is normal or expected. solution,

Life is supposed to be fun if it's not fun, I'm not doing it.

honor thy mother and father,

good intention treat your parents with respect and be grateful for them conditioned fear overly concerned about disappointing your parents or that you will be disowned if you follow your heart potential limits holding yourself back from what you want and know you need to do or who you are because your parents or others do not approve. Solution,

Instead of saying honor, thy mother and father.say I respect my mother and father's opinions of me, but

My parents will always love me and be there for me to the best of their ability. I have to love myself first, and that means knowing who I am and acting on what I love no matter what anyone else thinks.

no one ever said life is fair,

Good intention sometimes things seem unfair, but it is OK condition fear you will not get what you deserve and there is no justice in the world. Potential limits you may hold yourself back feeling like it will not pay off or you may develop feelings of hopelessness. Solution, tell yourself this instead

The universe is abundant cause and affect says that what I put out I get back it's guaranteed success that I will always be successful if I act on my highest excitement.

good things come to those who wait,

Good intention it is important to be patient

and it's worth the wait. Condition fear you have to wait a long time to get what you want. Potential limits a feeling of impatients due to focusing on the length of time and not doing something you want because it will take too long.

You have to pay your dues,

good intention of takes effort to get results condition for you will have to suffer in order to be worthy of any payoff potential limits feeling un-worthy you may not take opportunities or you may punish yourself a rewards in accomplishments you receive with ease.

Speak only one spoken to you,

good intention be polite and don't interrupt conditioned fear apprehension to approach others are speak up potential limits avoidance of activities are circumstances requiring you to be an authority, Lee demand what you want, stand up for what you believe, or speak in front of others.

Children are meant to be seen and not heard,

good intentions really there is no good inten-tion here condition for your feelings of being un-worthy and low self-esteem, potential limits avoidance of being in the spotlight or anything that would make you feel important or valued.

The last two were big ones of mine an example after you become mindful and aware of these things they don't block you anymore a belief is just something you keep thinking so stop giving it power and it will stop from blocking you in your life you can reprogram your mind with things that can help you grow and take your personal power back.

Like the examples of the solutions I gave. All you have to do after becoming aware of a limiting belief that you have is say the positives either after you say the limiting belief or after you notice you're about to say that limiting belief reprogramming your mind takes practice, but it can be done with awareness.

#8 STEP AFFIRMATIONS

Now you can reprogram yourself after you release what's been blocking you or holding you back you can listen to affirmations there's so many on YouTube you can find for free or you can make your own then in the morning in a mirror you can say I am statements make a list of all the things you would like to feel about yourself don't be shy or hold back put all the best things in your affirmations. There is never one way to do anything. so my affirmations won't work for you that's why you have to create your own. They have to resonate with you and who you want to be or who you are. Very powerful to look yourself in the mirror and use this as your daily practice it really works to establish your confidence again and to experience self love.

#9 STEP Self Discovery

self discovery is about learning who you are. And asking yourself a lot of questions. so you can discover your purpose, and that You are Energy in motion. Some tools that I used, but are not limited to are astrology, numerology, tarot, ruins, books personality quizzes, personality assessments, past life regression, human design report, Hypnosis with a professional of course. What did you like to do as a child ?what was your favorite game to play? What were you naturally good at? What did you never learn about yourself and your talents that you never saw in yourself? Or maybe you didn't see what were you naturally good at. Or maybe you did what was it ? For example when I was a kid before the age of three I just knew I liked to be on stage my mom put me in a beauty pageant at two years old. Also an elementary school I was good at selling stuff for school Fundraisers or for Girl Scouts. I liked to win the biggest prizes and to go on stage to get the prizes. I feel it was to be seen since I was a middle child and also experienced being told by my parents that limiting belief that children are to be seen and not heard. I always wanted to be on stage or being heard I did choir all the way to my senior year . What did you want to be when you grew up? I wanted to be a fashion designer, but only because my mom wouldn't let me pick out my own clothes after I was able to pick out my own clothes, being a fashion designer wasn't something I wished to do. What ended up being more important to me, was to be of service and to help others in anyway I could. I just didn't know what that would be until I got spiritually connected through self discovery journey by finding my blueprint in astrology, which didn't come until I was 21 I discovered that I wanted to be a teacher, but I didn't know a teacher of what, until now after looking back at my spiritual journey and learning the blueprint, I know that I love to teach from my experiences. So You see how researching yourself in greater detail can give you the words to Describe who you are in a clear aligned way that resonates with you deeply then after Learning, what makes you feel alive and connected deeply to your heart center you can ask yourself are you living your purpose now and if not why not ?

#10 STEP Living in JOY

living your joy means only doing things you enjoy trying your best to always be conscious of your feelings. Chasing your highest excitement at all times. Following your highest passion, Being totally present and enjoying your life to its fullest. No matter what. Down to doing chores if you don't enjoy it figure out a way to pay someone else to do it. Or do it later when you feel more motivated or inspired to do them. Just try to only do things you enjoy. Learn to say no to people when it's really not something you want to do. You're going to be happier and avoid unwanted stress in your life if you only do things you enjoy. Your Making your life harder than it needs to be by not acting on your highest excitement. Pay Attention to your desires at all times. Set boundaries with others that's having more self-love Choose to be happy like you chose to do drugs. Happiness is a choice, The Same effort you put into getting high put that same amount of effort to discover what makes you happy so you can live in a state of joy more often. Which is a higher Consciousness, state of being to live in and experience more things flowing to you effortlessly getting out of your own way, and not blocking the success that is trying to come to you.

#11 STEP Create your movie

Create your movie is becoming a producer of your own life story. Telling a new story What it will look like one year from now you can also do five years from now. Then read it back to yourself and have somebody else read it to you it's very powerful to hear somebody else read your story to you it hits differently. Once a month also reread it to yourself until you start seeing things take place you are man-ifesting your life to look like this. You are the creator of your story and your reality all you have to do is get clear on what you want and desire. put details in there, write people that are involved all your senses, what you were seeing daily what you are tasting the things you're eating what you are feeling in the moment in each regular day-to-day activities that you're doing how you are able to help give back to society what your bank account looks like the restaurants you're eating at maybe you don't like to clean so you have a housekeeper what serv-ice are you using?ect. You can do this once a year. What would you like to create or experience?

#12 STEP self love

Self love from my perspective means to get up early go to bed early drink lots of water. Water is life! Know thyself so you know what energy is yours and what is not because self love to me is caring today how I feel if some thing doesn't feel good then I'm not doing it or I'm not gonna be around it (setting boundaries)with people That don't know how to live life caring about how they feel. Being The main character on your story, giving energy and attention connecting to that inner child inside you and checking in daily asking yourself questions .Balancing your mind body and soul meditate daily practice different ways to meditate make it more fun and find what works for you. There's never only one way to do anything but you need to make a routine that works for you. Also Work out daily however, that looks for you I like to work out on a pole in my own home. I call it Pole Aerobics. Go get health check ups dentist check ups and cleanings. Do Things that you stop doing because you were high. Chase your highest excitement, your passions in life. Cut toxic people out of your life. Also another way to start over change your phone number changing your phone number is a sign of you starting over and moving on. Actually moving to a further destination from anywhere your addiction was taking place. Know your triggers. so that way you can avoid them. My triggers are smoking cigarettes because when I would smoke other stuff cigarettes would go good with them or another trigger break ups. so if and when I would break off friendships or relationships with lovers, I would make sure to reach out to other people so I wasn't alone Also, I chose to not date anyone for a year, so I was more emotionally stable because that was one of my main triggers to relapse in the past . Another trigger of mine was being around old neighborhoods so I would drive around those neighborhoods or not visit them at all. Being accountable to make good choices, New choices that keep you loving yourself and staying sober being disciplined and accountable and consistent. Always make sure you're taking care of yourself first paying yourself first because if you're not loving yourself and taking care of yourself first you're no good to anybody else or being of service for anybody else. Your needs always need to be put first before anyone else's. Put yourself first and everything else in life falls into place it's not selfish to put yourself first it's called self-love.

I do these 12 steps consistently after I had 20 years of using I have 3 years clean no relapse, no cravings, right now at the time of writing this book, and I have not had any thoughts of relapse. I have accomplished taking my personal power back by using these steps and they will work for you too. Life still has ups and downs but the downs are not that long anymore. I bounce back pretty quickly because I am fully aware of my personal power to make better choices. Life just gets easier when you're co creating it with your higher self. Which when I was using, I was not aware of the unseen team that I was connected to, and the love and support that I always had. and now that I am fully aware and connected, I live with unconditional love (loving without conditions)

And growing Every day, being a better version of myself today than I was yesterday.

Thank you for being a part of my story and allowing me to share how I changed my life from my darkest moments and brought light (truth) to how I became a life coach

please subscribe on my YouTube channels to get more Messages that can Maybe help you get Clarity and alignment on your spiritual journey as well

(Kelly Keith Goddess coach)

Also my other Channel

(Kelly Keith voice channeler)

If you would like a private session

My website is unitylovelifecoaching.com

KELLY KEITH

9 798886 830583